PART II – FIRST AID

PART III – AFTER THE EMERGENCY

About the Author

Charles T. P. Bell graduated from Cambridge University with a degree in Veterinary Medicine. He has practised for several years in both the United Kingdom and the United States, working with small animals.

Preface

It is my wish that no animal or animal owner ever be confronted with a "life or death" situation. However, accidents do happen all too frequently. If your cat suffers an injury, you may have to make several decisions very quickly. Often your choices will affect your pet's overall well-being. *First Aid & Health Care for Cats* was written to help you make the right decisions.

No book can take the place of your veterinary surgeon. In the time of a crisis, the best chance for a favourable outcome is to get your cat to your vet as quickly as possible. You should not waste time trying to diagnose or to treat your pet's injury. However, there are some basic steps that you can take that might stabilize the animal, reducing the chance of further damage and complications. These are the procedures advocated in this book.

First Aid & Health Care for Cats works as a bridge between your veterinary surgeon and you. The two of you are partners who share the same goal: maintaining the good health of your cat. This is the best way to ensure that your cat will enjoy a long, happy life. The book can also help prepare you to make the right choices for decisions that, hopefully, you will never have to make.

The book is divided into three parts.

Part I – Health Care

Part I outlines the various components of a general health care programme. These components are important to the maintenance of the overall good health of your cat. A healthy cat is in the best position to fight off disease and the effects of injuries. In addition, proper health care for your pet will reduce the chance of the animal transmitting a parasite or disease to other members of your family.

Part II–First Aid

This section outlines the first aid procedures that should be taken in many of the most common emergency situations. The steps described emphasize common sense, simplicity and your own safety.

Each chapter begins with a short overview that gives background information about the emergency. Next are the common signs that you are likely to see. These are followed by the proper steps to take. Just as important as telling you what to do, the book indicates what you should NOT do; it informs you of the common mistakes that people often make. Most chapters end by advising you to take your injured pet to your veterinary surgeon; Chapter 23 details the correct manner to do this.

The layout of each chapter facilitates quick and easy use. In the time of a crisis, you will not have to waste time searching for the proper steps to take.

Part III–After the Emergency

Your veterinary surgeon may ask you to take an active role in the recuperative process. This section instructs you how to administer medicine, check devices used for healing and deal with various issues associated with surgery.

Writing a book is a difficult task. Without the help and guidance of many individuals, this project would not have been completed. I would like to thank all of the reviewers (both the veterinary surgeons and the non-veterinary surgeons) for their comments. They forced me to filter out my own medical biases as well as to keep the material readily accessible to the intended audience. A special debt of gratitude goes to Alice Dworkin, whose advice pointed me in the right direction and comments kept me on course throughout the project.

I would also like to thank A. Christine MacMurray, Editor at the Animal Medical Center in New York City, for allowing me to access the AMC's library while researching the material.

Lastly, Karen Fortgang of Bookworks deserves credit for patiently guiding me through the various stages of production.

I would like to close with a word of warning. An injured animal can be a dangerous animal. A cat in pain may resist any handling and may lash out at you. You must be on guard and take precautions to protect yourself. If you are bitten or injured you should seek medical attention.

PART I

HEALTH CARE

1. Preventive Medicine

Introduction

Preventive medicine is taking steps to prevent illness. By following a complete programme, you help your cat maintain good health throughout its life. The most important aspects of a preventive medicine programme are a well-balanced diet and regular veterinary examinations. Chapter 2 discusses nutrition (see page **26**). Other components of preventive medicine are outlined below.

Going to your Veterinary Surgeon

Regular trips to your veterinary surgeon are crucial to the maintenance of your cat's health. Your vet can design a programme geared specifically for your cat. Periodic examinations will allow the veterinary surgeon to monitor your cat's progress and adjust the programme as needed. In addition, your vet will know of special issues that apply to your geographic location (such as the length of the flea and tick season or the prevalence of certain diseases).

You should visit your veterinary surgeon for a number of reasons.

- It is often easier to prevent a disease than to treat it. Your cat is better off if steps are taken to prevent an illness rather than if steps are needed to treat one. Some diseases cannot be cured, such as feline leukaemia.
- It is less expensive to prevent a disease than

to treat it. Vaccinations may seem expensive, but they are much cheaper than a cure for an illness. The money spent on preventive medicine is like buying insurance against disease; it is the best insurance policy available for your pet.

• Your cat may not be the only one who gets sick. Some of the diseases that threaten your cat can be transmitted to humans and to other animals. Taking steps to keep your cat disease-free is important to the overall health of the entire family.

Your first trip to your veterinary surgeon should be soon after obtaining your cat or kitten. This is the best time to begin a complete health programme. After the first series of visits, your cat should be examined by your vet at least once each year.

When Going to your Veterinary Surgeon

• Transport your cat in a catbox. There may be several animals at the clinic. You must be able to protect your cat as well as keep it under control.

• Try to remember any recent unusual behaviour exhibited by your cat. Give the veterinary surgeon as many details as you can.

Vaccinations

Vaccinations are powerful tools that stimulate the immune system, the natural line of defence against disease. Once a virus or bacterium has been

introduced and fought off, the immune system
remembers it and develops a mechanism to fight it
in the future. A vaccine is made from the same
agent that causes a disease but the agent is altered
so that it is harmless. The immune system, however, cannot tell the difference between the real
agent and the vaccine. This allows the body to
build up a defence to the disease without being
subjected to it.

Most vaccinations are given when your cat is young.
Kittens should receive 2 to 4 injections a few weeks
apart. Staging the vaccinations allows your kitten to
gradually build up adequate immunity. Until it has
received all of them your kitten may not be fully
protected. Annual booster vaccinations are needed
to keep the immune system strong.

Diseases Prevented by Vaccinations

- **Feline Leukaemia:** This is the most
  dangerous virus, accounting for most disease-
  related deaths of cats. The virus is linked to
  many serious illnesses including leukaemia,
  cancer and anaemia. It can also lead to a
  suppressed immune system. By breaking
  down the body's natural defences, it may
  result in the development of such secondary
  problems as chronic gum infection, fever,
  miscarried pregnancies and kidney problems.

  Feline leukaemia can exhibit a "time bomb"
  effect. A cat might be infected for many years
  before it shows any clinical signs of illness.
  Throughout this period it may be able to
  transmit the virus to other cats. This disease

can be prevented by an initial series of vaccinations followed by annual booster injections.

- **Feline Panleukopenia:** This virus attacks the intestinal tract and can cause severe diarrhoea, vomiting and dehydration. Depite treatment this disease frequently results in death.

  A panleukopenia vaccination usually includes vaccines for the feline calici virus and the feline herpes virus, which are the most common causes of respiratory disease in cats. In some countries, a vaccine against chlamydial conjunctivitis is also added. Symptoms of respiratory disease include sneezing, conjunctivitis, debilitation and fever. They may permanently damage the respiratory system and can be life threatening.

- **Rabies:** This is one of the most feared diseases for which there is no cure. Rabies attacks the brain and the nervous system. The United Kingdom is rabies-free. Therefore, there is no routine vaccination programme. However, there are very strict quarantine regulations for animals entering the UK.

Neutering

Neutering is the removal of the reproductive organs, preventing a cat from breeding. While this helps control the cat population it has medical and behavioural benefits as well. Neutering does not alter the personality of your cat.

- **Males:** Neutering of males is known as castration; it is the removal of the testicles. The most common time to have a male cat castrated is around the age of 6 months.

Advantages of Castration

- Prevents unwanted pregnancies and kittens
- Often causes cat to be less aggressive (less likely to fight)
- Less likely to wander off thereby reducing its chance of being hit by a car
- Less likely to spray in the house. (Spraying is the type of urination used to mark territory)
- Urine odour is greatly reduced

Disadvantages of Castration

- Cannot breed
- Has to have an operation, requiring general anaesthesia
- May tend to gain weight (easily controlled by adjusting diet)

- **Females:** Neutering of females is known as spaying. This is the removal of the ovaries and uterus. The most common time to have a female spayed is around the age of 6 months.

Advantages of Spaying

- Prevents unwanted pregnancies and kittens
- Greatly reduces the risk of mammary cancer if performed early in life
- Eliminates the risk of pyometra, a very serious disease that involves the production of pus in the uterus
- Eliminates annoying behaviour associated with going into "heat," such as repeated crying

Disadvantages of Spaying

- Cannot breed
- Has to have an operation requiring general anaesthesia
- May tend to gain weight (easily controlled by adjusting diet)

Unless you plan to breed from your cat, you should elect to have it neutered. The risk caused by anaesthesia and surgery is very low (especially for a young cat) and is outweighed by the medical and social benefits.

Parasites

There are a number of parasites that can affect your cat. These include worms, fleas, ticks and mange mites. They are discussed in Chapter 3.

Environment

Cats are fastidious animals; they constantly clean themselves and prefer a clean environment. They also like privacy; the litter box should be placed in a secluded location that is separate from the feeding area. You should change the kitty litter and clean the bedding at least once a week. Stools in the litter box should be removed every day; it is advisable to wear gloves when doing so. These steps will decrease the chances that your cat or your family will contract parasites or diseases.

Skin Care

Good skin care helps prevent skin problems. These are usually difficult to treat and can lead to infection if a cat constantly bites or scratches itself. Once a cat has had a skin problem it is often prone to contracting another.

All cats should be regularly brushed. Long-haired cats should be brushed every day. This removes mats and knots and reduces the chance of hairballs (clumps of ingested hair). In addition, regular brushing allows you to closely examine your cat, increasing the chance of early detection of problems. You should use a comb and brush designed specifically for cats.

Other steps may be required; your veterinary surgeon can best advise you on how to care for your cat. Some suggestions are listed below.

- **Dietary Supplements:** There are several food supplements that can help your cat's skin. Any supplement should be designed specifically for cats. Oversupplementation can be harmful; check with your veterinary surgeon before beginning to use one.

- **Fleas:** Fleas should be treated quickly. They cause the cat to scratch and can lead to skin infection. Fleas are discussed in greater detail in Chapter 3.

Care of Teeth and Gums

The care of teeth and gums is becoming increasingly recognized as important for general good health. Cats with dental problems may develop bad breath and may go off their food. Poor dental care may lead to inflamed and infected gums, which in turn may result in loss of teeth. There is a chance that infection will enter the bloodstream where it may affect internal organs such as the kidneys. Bad teeth and gums are especially debilitating for older animals. Consult with your veterinary surgeon as to what steps you should take to foster good teeth and gums.

Example of a Complete Health Programme

The following is an example of a complete health programme for your cat. Such a programme should take into account many variables including the type of cat, type of vaccine, climate and other regional issues. These factors can change from time to time. As such, your veterinary surgeon is in the best position to design a programme that is suited to the specific needs of your cat. The two of you should work together to set it up.

Kitten

Soon after Acquisition:
- Complete examination by your veterinary surgeon

8 to 10 Weeks:
- Combined Panleukopenia and flu vaccination
- Feline leukaemia test
- Treat for worms

10 to 12 Weeks
- Combined Panleukopenia and flu vaccination
- Feline leukaemia vaccination
- Treat for worms

12 to 14 Weeks
- Feline leukaemia vaccination
- Treat for worms

Adult

Daily
- Brush/comb out cat
- Supplement food, if necessary (check with your veterinary surgeon)

Weekly
- Weigh cat

Every 3 Months
- Treat for worms

Yearly
- Complete examination by your veterinary surgeon
- Combined Panleukopenia and flu vaccination
- Feline leukaemia vaccination

- Treat for worms
- Geriatric clinical investigation (older cats only

Summary

- Preventive medicine is a crucial concern for the health of both your cat and your entire family.
- You should visit your veterinary surgeon soon after acquiring your kitten or cat.
- Your veterinary surgeon should examine your cat at least once a year.
- Vaccinations help the immune system to fight off specific diseases.
- Unless you plan to breed from your cat, you should have it castrated or spayed.
- Care of teeth and gums is an essential part of preventive medicine.

2. Nutrition

Introduction

Excellent health begins with good nutrition. The keys to good nutrition are plenty of fresh water and the correct quantity of a well-balanced diet.

Fresh Water

It is crucial that your cat always has access to fresh, clean water. Without sufficient water, it may dehydrate, leading to a wide variety of problems. It is a good idea to make water available in several areas of your home and to change the water daily. Adequate water is especially important for older cats.

What to Feed

A well-balanced diet begins with the correct food. It is best to use a quality commercial diet which can be bought at supermarkets, pet stores or from your veterinary surgeon. Commercial food companies have spent years perfecting the composition of their foods. The result is that these foods provide the best mix of nutrients and flavour. A home-made diet can be well-balanced, but it will probably be more expensive than a good commercial brand and it may leave out important nutrients.

The food that you select should be designed specifically for cats. Even though it is generally less expensive than cat food, dog food should not be given to cats. Cats have significantly different nutritional requirements; for example, they need a higher level of protein. Dog food does not provide a well-balanced diet for cats.

Once you have decided on a type of food do not change often. A cat's digestive system does not adapt well to sudden change which may cause diarrhoea. However, your cat would probably enjoy a wide variety of tastes. Many types of cat food come in different flavours.

Milk is not necessary for a cat's health. Some do not tolerate it and it is a common cause of diarrhoea. But if your cat enjoys the taste and does not suffer any ill effects, milk can be given. Some manufacturers market a 'cat' milk, which is cow's milk changed in composition to make it tolerable to cats.

It is important to clean the water and feed bowls on a regular basis. Also food must be stored properly after it has been opened; instructions for this are usually written on the package. Any food that appears mouldy or has a rancid odour should be discarded.

Types of Food Available

There are three main types of cat food available today.

Dry
- Low moisture (stays fresh in feed bowl)
- Inexpensive
- Convenient

Semi-moist
- Stays fresh in bowl for several hours
- Often not good as a total diet; best given as a supplement

Canned Meat
- Very palatable and nutritious
- Usually the most expensive
- Will not stay fresh very long in bowl

Several factors should be considered when selecting the best food for your cat. A few are listed below.

- Age of cat (kitten, adult or older cat)
- Cat's individual quirks (will eat anything or very finicky)
- Cost of food

Special Diets

There are special diets available to assist in the treatment or management of important medical conditions, such as kidney disease, heart disease, feline urological syndrome and other urinary problems, obesity and several others. Your veterinary surgeon can determine if your cat has a condition that may respond to dietary modification and recommend the best product. While many "light" foods are available to help promote weight loss, you should not make a change in diet without first consulting your veterinary surgeon.

How Much to Feed

Most cat foods have a feeding chart on the package. However, this chart should be used only as a rough guideline. Each cat is different; some need more food than others. By experimenting with various portions of food, you will eventually determine the best amount for your cat. Your veterinary surgeon should be consulted on this matter.

How Often to Feed

A guideline for how often to feed is given below. Again, remember not all cats are the same. Your veterinary surgeon can help you determine the proper feeding schedule.

- Up to 4 months of age — feed 4 times a day
- Aged 4 to 6 months — feed 3 times a day
- Older than 6 months — feed 2 times a day

Most adult cats do better if fed twice daily rather than only once. Some will eat their food so fast that they make themselves sick. For a cat such as this, you might feed it the same amount of food but split the portions up into smaller quantities and feed more often. In addition, you may want to leave out a dry snack food throughout the day. These snack foods, however, are not designed to be the sole source of nutrients; they are not well-balanced. If your cat snacks to the point that it loses interest in its main diet, you should limit the amount of food between meals.

Controlling Weight

Ideal weight varies with each individual cat. Your veterinary surgeon and you can determine the best weight for your cat. Once this has been established, you can help your cat maintain that weight through periodic evaluations. Two methods are outlined below.

Measuring by Touch

- Stand the cat up
- Place hands on opposite sides of the rib cage. Cat is overweight if you cannot feel the ribs at all

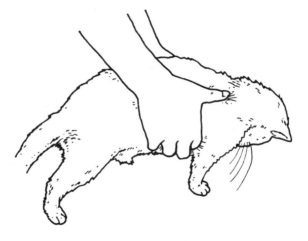

- Feel for the spines of the vertebrae in the lower back. Cat is underweight if these are readily detectable

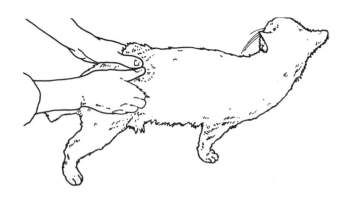

- Cat is ideal if you can just feel each rib and there is good muscle depth on either side of the back bone

Measuring by Weighing

- Weigh the cat and yourself on a bathroom scale
- Set the cat down
- Weigh yourself alone
- Subtract your weight from that of the cat and you combined. The difference is the weight of the cat

If your cat is too thin, you should increase the amount of food given at the main meals. You might also supplement its diet with a dry snack food. If it still does not gain weight, your cat should be examined by your veterinarian. An older cat that is losing weight should be taken to your vet. If your cat is overweight, take steps to help it lose weight.

Losing Weight

Obesity is by far the most common nutritional problem in cats. An overweight cat is a walking time bomb. Obesity contributes to such long-term illnesses as heart disease, diabetes and certain forms of cancer. In addition, lugging around the extra weight is uncomfortable (especially in hot weather). You can help your cat lose weight.

Steps for Weight Loss

- Reduce amount of food given per day by a third
- Change regular food to a special diet food
- Eliminate all snacks

Dieting for cats can be dangerous, just as it can be for people. You should consult your veterinary surgeon before taking any step that may cause your cat to lose weight.

Food Supplements

There are several types of supplements that are helpful to your cat's health. It is important to stick to the recommended dosage. Over-supplementation can be harmful.

- **Vitamins:** Kittens and older cats often need more nutrients than younger adults. Vitamins designed specifically for cats can meet this need. However, consult your vet before using them.

- **Snack foods:** Discussed in "How Often to Feed" section. These can be good as long as your cat does not lose interest in the main meals.

- **Bones:** These are not good for cats. A swallowed bone is not easily digestible and can lead to stomach and intestinal problems. It might have to be taken out by surgery.

- **Oils:** Certain oils can be added to the regular food. Oils help make the coat healthy and shiny. They can also make the food taste better. There are several products available through veterinary surgeons and pet stores that make good oil supplements. Small amounts of corn oil and olive oil (1/4 to 1/2 teaspoon a day) are also good. If your cat starts producing soft stools, reduce the amount of oil given.

Table Scraps

Table scraps are not good for a cat. They often upset the stomach, causing vomiting and diarrhoea. In addition, they are the leading cause of obesity and foster annoying behaviour such as begging.

Summary

- Always have clean, fresh water available.
- Choose a commercial cat food that provides a complete, balanced diet.
- Do not change the type of food often.
- Adjust the amount of food given to suit your cat's needs.
- Adjust the number of meals a day to suit your cat's needs.
- Regularly check your cat's weight.
- Supplements can be good for your cat.
- Do not feed your cat table scraps.

3. Parasites

Introduction

A parasite is an organism that lives off another organism to the detriment of the host. A number of parasites affect cats. Besides being debilitating to animals, some can affect people. As soon as parasites are detected on a cat, it should be treated promptly and thoroughly.

Worms

There are many types of worms. Some of the more common are discussed below.

- **Roundworm:** Look like short, thin spaghetti. Can cause vomiting, diarrhoea, weight loss and lack of growth in kittens.

  If your cat is heavily infected, worms may be seen in vomit or stools. Cat to cat transmission occurs via the ingestion of soiled material, faeces or milk (from the mother when kittens are suckling). Infection can be transmitted to humans through ingestion of soiled material and faeces.

- **Tapeworm:** Look like rice grains attached to the anus. Can be fairly mobile and may move around by changing their shape in a slow motion manner.

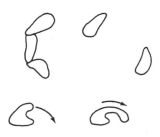

These worms usually do not show any clinical signs in your cat but can cause diarrhoea and weight loss in some cases. Infection is transmitted by ingestion of an infected flea or of wild animals such as mice and rats. Humans can also be infected if a flea is swallowed (cannot be transmitted directly from the cat).

There are several signs to look for if you think that your cat might have worms.

Signs of Worms

- Vomiting and/or diarrhoea
- Pot-bellied abdomen (mainly in kittens)
- Loss of weight (even if eating more food than normal)
- Spaghetti-like particles in vomit or faeces
- Rice-like particles around the anus
- Anal irritation

What to Do

- Take your cat to your veterinary surgeon for an examination

Your cat will be treated with an injection and/or oral medicine. Treatment is usually carried out in two stages. The first stage will kill the existing worms but not their eggs. The second kills the recently hatched worms before they can breed. The timing between the two is crucial; follow your veterinary surgeon's instructions diligently.

You can minimize the chance of your cat contracting worms.

Steps of Prevention

- Clean the litter box often. Wear gloves when doing so
- Do not let your cat eat mice or rats
- Routinely worm your cat every 3 months with a wormer supplied by your veterinary surgeon
- Treat for fleas as needed

Other Intestinal Parasites

Besides worms, other parasites affect the intestinal tract. Signs, treatment and prevention of these are similar to that of worms.

- **Coccidia:** Tiny parasite that lives in the intestinal tract; seen only through a microscope. Can cause diarrhoea (occasionally with blood), weight loss and dehydration. Transmitted by ingestion of faecal-contaminated material.

- **Giardia:** Also a microscopic parasite living in the intestines. Similar symptoms and characteristics to those of coccidia. Can be transmitted to people.

- **Toxoplasma:** Microscopic parasite that migrates through body tissue. It can produce a wide variety of symptoms and can affect virtually any organ. But it is often carried without showing any clinical signs.

Toxoplasma can infect people. Those most at risk are people who have impaired immune systems, such as those undergoing chemotherapy or those with AIDS. In addition, it has been known to migrate through the placenta of pregnant women and cause birth defects or miscarriages. Therefore, pregnant women should be especially hygenic.

While the parasite is usually transmitted by eating undercooked meat, it can also be transmitted through the ingestion of cat faeces or faecal-contaminated food. Infected cats excrete the parasite in the form of cysts in their faeces. In order to become infective to people, the cysts must mature. This process can take from 12 hours to 5 days after excretion of the contaminated faeces.

Steps can be taken to prevent toxoplasmosis.
- A blood test can be taken from your cat to test for antibodies against the parasite.
- A faecal test can also be taken.
- Only feed your cat a commercial diet. The manufacturing process will kill the parasite.
- Restrict hunting to a minimum.
- Clean the litter box twice a day.
  - Wear rubber gloves.
  - Pregnant woman and immuno-suppressed people should not clean the litter box.
- Wash hands thoroughly before eating as well as before and after preparing meats and vegetables.
- People who think that they may be at risk should check with their doctor.

Ringworm

Contrary to its name, ringworm is not a worm; it is a fungus that causes skin disease. It is transmitted by contact with an infected cat or its environment. Common sites of ringworm are animal shelters and other locations where large groups of animals are kept. Kittens are most commonly affected; ringworm can infect people as well, particularly children.

Signs of Ringworm

- Hair loss in patches
- Lesions around the eyes, ears, head and feet
- Scaling and crusting of the skin
- Excessive scratching

What to Do

• Consult your veterinary surgeon

Fleas

The most likely reason that a cat scratches itself is that it has fleas. Fleas are insects often seen running or jumping around an infected animal. They feed by biting the animal and sucking its blood.

Fleas are harmful in two ways. Firstly, they often cause skin infections. Flea bites itch; heavy scratching irritates the skin making it more susceptible to infection. Some cats are allergic to flea bites. Thus, one bite alone can lead to a serious skin problem. Secondly, fleas feed on blood. When biting through the skin, they can transmit diseases into the bloodstream. Both of these problems can affect people as well. A heavy flea infestation can cause anaemia, which occasionally can be fatal (especially for kittens).

Fleas thrive in warm weather. As such, they are a year-round problem in warm climates. While prevalent mainly during the summer months in cold climates, fleas can continue to live indoors if the temperature inside is constantly warm. They can infest even the cleanest home.

In order to control fleas, you must treat both the cat and the cat's environment. Fleas can move quickly and easily. If you treat the cat but not the home, garden and bedding the problem will persist. Also, if you have more than one animal you should treat them all at the same time.

There are a number of good products available for controlling fleas. Your veterinary surgeon can tell you which products work best in your area.

Flea Control

- Use a flea and tick powder or spray designed for cats once a week. It is important to read the product label and to follow the instructions carefully; incorrect use can lead to poisoning. Small kittens may need special treatment; check with your veterinary surgeon first.
- Use a flea and tick collar. This will limit the number of fleas but may not totally control them. Check the neck once a week for any signs of skin reaction.
- Medication designed to be applied monthly to your cat's skin is now available. This soaks into the system and the fleas die when they bite the cat. No other anti-flea product should be used with this on your cat.
- Treat your home and garden with a top-quality flea control product.
- Wash the cat's bedding once a week.

Ticks

Ticks are large parasites that feed by sucking blood. They bury their heads in the skin (usually around the head, neck and ear areas) and are difficult to remove. Since they penetrate the skin, they can transmit diseases such as Lyme disease. Lyme disease is a bacterial disease that can cause fever, lethargy, heart problems, kidney failure, meningitis and sore joints. It can affect people as well, but it is usually transmitted directly from the deer tick.

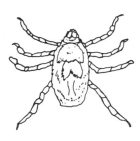

The tick season occurs in warm weather. During this time you should examine your cat every time it comes in from outside. If you see a tick, remove it at once.

Tick Control

- Use a flea and tick collar
- Use a flea and tick powder once a week
- Examine the cat when it comes in from outside

What to Do — Removing a Tick

- Spray a heavy dose of flea spray directly on the tick or cover it with strong alcohol. Be careful not to get any spray or alcohol into your cat's mouth, nose, eyes or ear canal.
- Wait 5 minutes.
- Pull tick off using a pair of tweezers. (Do not use your fingers; direct contact with a tick may increase the chance of you contracting a disease from it.)
  - Grasp tick as close to the skin as possible.
  - Pull using a steady, even pressure. Do not use a sudden jerk or twist.

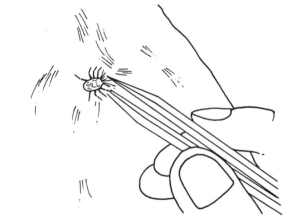

- Contact your veterinary surgeon if you have any problems. The most common problem is leaving the head of the tick in the skin; this often leads to infection.

Ear Mites

Ear mites are tiny parasites that affect cats in two ways. Firstly, they cause itching which, when alleviated by heavy scratching, can lead to ruptured blood vessels. Secondly, the mites cause the ear to secrete a thick waxy discharge that often clogs the ear canal. Both can lead to ear infection. Mites are transmitted by direct contact with infected animals; this often happens to kittens still in the litter and to outdoor cats.

Steps To Control Ear Mites

- Have cat or kitten examined by your vet soon after acquisition
- Have the ears examined if there is persistent scratching
- Follow the directions for treatment given by your veterinary surgeon. The proper way to administer ear medication is shown in Chapter 24

Mange

The many varieties of mange are caused by mites that burrow into the skin or that live in the hair or on the skin surface. They are most often found around the head, neck, eyes or ears. They can cause a tremendous amount of scratching, making the skin susceptible to infection. Some forms of mange can be transmitted to people.

Signs of Mange

- Heavy scratching
- Loss of hair
- Dry, scaly skin over parts of the body
- Sores covering parts of the body

What to Do

- Consult your veterinary surgeon.

Summary

- It is not uncommon for a cat to have parasites.
- Parasites can be a health hazard to people.
- All parasites should be eradicated as soon as detected.
- Worm your cat every 3 months with a wormer supplied by your vet.
- When controlling fleas, you must treat both the cat and the cat's environment.
- Successful flea treatment must be consistent and thorough.
- When removing a tick, contact your vet if you leave the head of the tick in the skin.
- Have your cat examined if there is persistent scratching.

4. Breeding your Cat

Introduction

Breeding your cat can be a very rewarding experience. To see a cat that you love bring a set of offspring into the world can be very gratifying. It can also be very educational if you have children in your household. A child that observes the birth of a litter of kittens will develop an understanding of how life is created.

However, breeding your cat also creates a great deal of responsibility. The kittens that your cat will bring to life will need homes. Finding a good home for each kitten in a litter is not an easy task, especially if the kittens are mixed breeds. In addition, most rescue shelters are full of cats that need homes. Unless you are successful at placing each kitten, you will very likely be adding to that sad number.

Preventing Unwanted Pregnancies

Allowing your cat to have a litter of kittens creates a lengthy time commitment. The gestation period for a cat is around 60-65 days; the kittens will not be ready to go to their new homes until they are 8-12 weeks of age. In total, the process from conception to rehoming will take approximately 5 months. Throughout that period you will have to contend with a mother who requires increased attention and a litter of kittens that will need constant monitoring. Unless you are willing to make that kind of commitment you should not let your cat become pregnant.

The best way to prevent your cat from becoming pregnant is to have her spayed at an early age. This was discussed in the chapter on Preventive Medicine (see page **19**). If your cat is not spayed, you should confine her whenever she goes into heat. That is the time when she is receptive to male cats and able to become pregnant. During this period, the animal should not be let outside without supervision. She will be attracting males from quite a distance; if she is not constantly watched a male may be able to obtain access to her and mate with her.

Caring for a Pregnant Cat

When your cat is pregnant, she will be undergoing many physical changes that will place a great deal of stress on her system. You will have to adjust her care to meet the new requirements. Around the sixth week, she will require an increase in her food intake. With the development of the kittens, her need for protein and energy will increase. This nutritional adjustment upward will continue to grow until it reaches its peak around the fourth week of lactation. At that point, your cat may need as much as 3 times her normal ration. You should discuss your cat's diet and your feeding practices with your veterinary surgeon. There are prescription diets available through vets that are designed to meet the specific requirements of pregnancy and lactation.

About 2 weeks before the end of the pregnancy you should start to make preparations for the birth of the kittens. It is a good idea to prepare a room where the kittens can be born. This should be a warm, quiet place that is dimly lit. It should be draught-free but not stuffy. The area should be confining but not cramped. This will simulate a cave, which many cats like. A cupboard underneath a staircase is often a good spot.

You should also be prepared to assist your cat. Near the site intended for the birth, you should place a large basket or box with plenty of clean towels. These can be used to help clean the kittens if the mother needs help or rejects them. For the same reason, it is a good idea to purchase a kitten milk replacer. There may be a few kittens that need extra nutritional assistance.

Birth

You may get a clue to the day on which your cat is likely to give birth. A few days before the event, your cat's mammary glands may begin to secrete milk. The process of giving birth can be divided into 3 stages. During the first stage, your cat may become restless, cry, pant, refuse food and frequently go in and out of her litter tray. She will probably exhibit nest-building behaviour and she will constantly rearrange her bedding. The length of this stage varies for each litter. However, once it begins, most cats will usually deliver their kittens within 24 hours.

In the second stage, your cat will experience powerful, rhythmic contractions of the abdominal muscles. Sometimes there is a green discharge from the vulva. The first kitten should arrive shortly after this. The time interval between each kitten being born is usually 10-60 minutes. However, some cats will give birth to half of the litter, rest for 12-24 hours before giving birth quite happily to the rest of their offspring.

Usually the mother will lick the kitten vigorously and tear off any membranes still attached to it. She will also break the umbilical cord. The kitten will then begin to feed by suckling.

The final stage involves expulsion of the placenta and foetal membranes. The timing of this stage varies with each cat. It can be immediately after the birth of a kitten or after the delivery of the next kitten. In some cases, however, there can be a time lag of up to 24 hours.

Throughout these stages, you should closely monitor your cat's progress. In most cases, you will not need to assist her. However, there are times when you should intervene. You should contact your veterinary surgeon if your cat has strong rhythmic contractions for 2 hours and yet fails to deliver a kitten. In addition, your vet should be informed if the cat's contractions start out strong but become progressively weaker and weaker with time. If a kitten gets stuck in the birth canal, you may be able to help it along by gently pulling it. If that does not free the kitten, you should call your veterinary surgeon for assistance.

If the mother neglects a kitten, you should clean it yourself. Begin by tearing off the membranes. You should clean the mouth and nostril area and then vigorously rub the kitten with a clean towel. Any fluid that is in the lungs can be drained by holding the kitten upside down and swinging it gently from side to side. You should break the umbilical cord if the mother has not done so herself within 5 minutes after delivery.

After the kitten is clean and the lungs are clear, you should check to see if it is lively. This can be done by placing your little finger in the kitten's mouth. This should elicit a strong suck reflex by the new-born animal. At this point the kitten is ready to be reintroduced to the mother by plugging it onto a nipple.

Orphan Kittens

In some cases, the mother may reject all contact with one or more of her kittens. These are known as orphan kittens. If the animal is to have a chance of surviving, you will have to intervene.

The first step is to place the kitten in a small box with a hot water bottle. The hot water bottle should be covered with a towel to protect the kitten from burns. You can provide additional warmth by covering the kitten with a towel as well. The kitten and the area where it is residing must be kept scrupulously clean.

You will need to feed the kitten every 2-3 hours. A special milk replacer can be obtained from your veterinary surgeon or pet shop. It is correctly balanced for new-born kittens. If a proper replacer is not available, you can make a temporary substitute by mixing cow's milk, cream and an egg yolk. A kitten should be switched to a proper replacer as soon as possible. It should not be on a homemade formula for more than a 24 hour period.

When feeding a kitten with a milk replacer you should use a syringe or a dropper. This will give the kitten access to the milk and allow you some control over the amount being fed. You should take care not to overfill the mouth. If that were to happen some of the mixture might get into the lungs.

After the Birth of the Litter

After all the kittens are cared for, the mother should be given a chance to rest. However, within a couple of days, it is a good idea to transport the entire family to your veterinary surgeon. The vet can ensure that your cat has come through the pregnancy and the process of giving birth in good shape. The veterinary surgeon can also evaluate the status of each kitten. You can then receive any special instructions for helping your cat and giving the kittens the best chance for survival.

Your cat will produce milk for 5-6 weeks. During this time, you should continue to monitor her health. Some mothers suffer from a condition called lactation tetany. This occurs when the calcium level in the mother's blood drops well below normal. It is caused by the kittens drinking so much milk that a severe calcium depletion develops. The mother may experience symptoms similar to that of a fit or seizure and may start to show muscle twitching and a rolling of the eyes. She might even collapse.

This is an emergency situation. The first step is to prevent the kittens from drawing off any more milk; you should separate your cat from her offspring. Then you should contact your veterinary surgeon immediately.

However, if no problems develop, the kittens will begin to wean themselves by eating bits of their mother's food. This can begin when the kittens are 3 weeks of age. By the time that they are 5-6 weeks old they should be introduced to a diet formulated specifically for kittens. Two to three weeks after that they will be ready to join their new homes.

Summary

- Breeding your cat can be rewarding but brings a tremendous responsibility.

- If you do not plan to breed your female cat she should be spayed.
- You should assist your cat through pregnancy by increasing her diet as necessary and by providing an area where she can build a nest for her litter.
- Most cats can deliver their kittens with no assistance from their owners.
- You should be prepared to assist your cat or her kittens if a complication develops.
- Shortly after the birth of the kittens, your cat and her offspring should be examined by your veterinary surgeon.
- You should continue to monitor your cat and the kittens throughout the lactation and weaning periods to ensure that all remain healthy.

5. The Older Cat

Introduction

As a cat ages, its body begins to lose the ability to fight off disease and to repair itself. An older cat can have an enjoyable and rewarding life, but this stage of life requires some adjustments. While this chapter will give you some ideas, your veterinary surgeon is the best source of information and advice.

Ageing

Every cat ages at a different rate. Some cats will show signs of ageing at about 8 years, others may not until they are 14 or 15 years old.

Signs of an Older Cat

- Less active than usual
- Changes in normal habits, such as sleeping more
- Changes in personality
- More sensitive to extremes of heat and cold

These are normal signs of ageing and should not alarm you (unless there is a sudden change). But you should discuss them with your veterinary surgeon on your next visit.

Older cats may have less effective immune systems making them more susceptible to disease and illness. In addition, the body organs do not function as well in an older cat as they do in a younger one. Some cats begin to have problems with their kidneys, heart, liver or thyroid glands. If any of the signs listed below appear, your cat should be examined by your veterinary surgeon.

Signs of Problems in an Older Cat

- Loss of weight
- Vomiting and diarrhoea
- Loss or increase in appetite
- Increased drinking and urination
- Pain
- Difficulty standing
- Difficulty breathing
- Bumping into objects
- Blood in urine
- Coughing
- Drooling
- Reduced sense of hearing

Loss of weight is a common sign in a cat slowly developing a disease. It is a good idea to weigh your cat once a week as it gets older. This will allow you to monitor any gradual changes.

Nutrition

The nutritional needs of an older cat are different from that of one in the prime of life. As a cat loses some of its energy, its need for food reduces and its ability to digest food may be impaired. Without a change in its diet, your cat may become overweight. Obesity compounds problems related to ageing. Changing the type of food may be a good idea. Several foods geared for the needs of older cats are available. In addition, there are foods designed for cats with specific problems, such as heart disease, kidney disease and bladder stones. Adding a vitamin supplement designed for cats may also be beneficial.

Above all, you should provide enough clean, fresh water in several locations. Many older cats suffer from kidney problems which may progress to kidney failure. The result is that more water than normal is released into the urine. Additional water is needed to replace the large amount voided by urinating. Inadaquate water intake may lead to dehydration. This can damage many internal organs, cause a build up of toxic by-products and potentially develop into a life-threatening condition.

Check with your veterinary surgeon before making any changes to your cat's diet or adding a supplement. Your vet has your cat's medical background and can help you make the best decisions.

The Geriatric Clinical Investigation

In older cats, many major problems and diseases develop slowly. Early diagnosis greatly increases the chance of successful treatment and management of problems. To help catch them early, many veterinary surgeons are now offering a "geriatric clinical investigation".

A geriatric clinical investigation is a series of tests and examinations that may show up a problem before serious symptoms develop. With the results, your veterinary surgeon can advise you on steps to take that will maximize your cat's good health and life expectancy. This investigation can become a regular component of your annual visit.

The following is an example of a very thorough clinical investigation illustrating the possibilities of modern veterinary medicine. The actual protocol chosen for your cat can vary tremendously depending on the result of the physical examination and your cat's medical history.

An Example of a Geriatric Clinical Investigation

- Complete physical examination
- X-ray of the chest
- X-ray of the abdomen
- Complete blood test
- Thyroid test
- Urine test
- Electrocardiogram

Summary

- Older cats can enjoy life and be happy.
- Signs of ageing are not serious unless there are signs of other problems.
- Loss of weight is a good clue that something is wrong.
- Changing your cat's diet may be advisable.
- Access to clean, fresh water in several locations is imperative for older cats.
- Do not switch to a special food or a supplement for an older cat before checking with your veterinary surgeon.
- A geriatric clinical investigation once a year may help head off problems.

6. Travelling with your Cat

Introduction

If you plan to visit another country, you should organize and prepare for the trip at least 3 months in advance. If leaving the UK for a holiday with a cat, it should be for at least a year – otherwise the cat will spend longer in quarantine than it will on holiday. There are several issues that need to be addressed before departure.

Travel Regulations and Procedures

Each country has very strict regulations concerning the importation of cats which must be adhered to precisely. The exact requirements differ with each country. These requirements can change often and without notice due to developments such as a sudden outbreak of a disease or an unexpected change in the political climate. There are several requirements in the United Kingdom regarding the export of a cat. In addition, once out of your own country, you will have to make sure that you follow the proper procedures in order to get your cat back home. Find out which documents are needed before leaving.

The strict requirements are intended to prevent the spread of diseases across international borders. An example of why these policies are so stringent involves rabies, a deadly disease that has no cure. At present, the United Kingdom is rabies-free. This has been achieved by imposing a strict, mandatory law that requires all animals brought into the country to be quarantined for a period of 6 months. If an animal had rabies it would exhibit symptoms within that time period. Those that are found to have the disease are euthanized. Those that are found to be healthy at the end of the quarantine period are allowed to enter the country.

Planning a Trip

If you are planning to take your cat across an international border, you should take a number of steps ahead of your departure. The first step is to find out the import requirements for each country that you will be visiting. Some countries have mandatory quarantine periods (at the owner's expense) and limitations to the age of cats that are allowed to enter. You should also find out the requirements for bringing your cat home. You can contact the Ministry of Agriculture or the equivalent for the various countries to learn their respective regulations. Failure to follow the proper procedures carries stiff penalties. Smuggling a cat across a border can result in a fine and/or imprisonment.

The next step is to contact your veterinary surgeon. In all likelihood, your cat will need to obtain a certificate that verifies its good health. This will show that your pet is up to date with all vaccinations, including one for rabies. Your vet can also advise you on precautions to guard your cat against any diseases or parasites that are prevalent in the areas that you are going to visit.

If you are planning to have your pet shipped across a border via a shipper or an airline, you should also contact your chosen carrier 3 months prior to your departure date. The shipper will know of the regulations concerning the movement of animals across the various borders. One of the prime considerations is the type of container to be used. There are very specific requirements regarding the size, construction material, number of ventilation holes and identification used. In addition, each shipper has its own policies governing the handling of animals. Many will not accept female cats that are in heat or cats that are under a specified age.

Given the number and variety of regulations that govern the import and export of a cat, it may be best to leave the animal at home with a friend looking after it or to place it in a reputable cattery.

The Day of Departure

If the cat will be accompanying you, you can get the trip off to a good start by following a few simple steps. Firstly, when your day of departure arrives, give your cat a light meal and a small drink of water 2 hours prior to travelling. In addition, make certain that the cat cannot interfere with the operation of your car. Confining it in a cat carrier is a good idea; one can be purchased from most pet shops. You should also be conscious of the heat when moving in slow traffic and parking your car. An animal can overheat in a very short period of time. Above all, never leave your cat in a parked car; the risk of heatstroke is too great (see page **107**).

One last point should be made. Many animals become nervous and anxious while travelling. If your cat is one of these, contact your veterinary surgeon before beginning your journey. This may be imperative if your cat is being shipped. The vet may prescribe a tranquilliser that will keep your pet quiet and comfortable while in transit.

Summary

- If you want to take your cat outside the UK, carefully plan your trip at least 3 months in advance.
- Find out the import and export regulations for animals in each country that you will be visiting.
- Find out what procedures will be required in order to bring your cat back into the United Kingdom.
- The smuggling of an animal across an international border is a serious offence that can lead to a fine and/or imprisonment.
- Consult your veterinary surgeon regarding necessary health documents and precautions to protect your cat while abroad.
- Discuss with your veterinary surgeon the steps to take to make your cat more comfortable while travelling.

PART II

FIRST AID

7. Essential Procedures

Overview

There are several basic procedures that you should know. These will allow you to monitor your cat's health between visits to the veterinary surgeon.

Weighing Your Cat

Obesity is a common problem among cats. Regular weighing will help you control your cat's weight.

What to Do

- Weigh the cat and yourself on a bathroom scale.
- Set the cat down.
- Weigh yourself alone.
- Subtract your weight from that of the cat and you combined. The difference is the weight of your cat.

Taking a Temperature

Normal temperature is 38.3-39°C (101-102°F). Use a rectal thermometer.

What to Do

- Shake the thermometer down to about 34-35°C (93-94°F).

- Lubricate the thermometer with petroleum jelly.
- Have somebody hold the cat.
- Raise and hold the tail.
- Using a gentle twisting motion, insert the thermometer approximately 2cm into the anus.

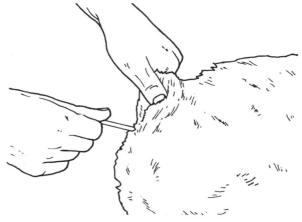

- Keep hold of both the thermometer and the tail.
- Leave in for 30 seconds to 1 minute.
- Pull out, wipe clean and read.

What NOT to Do

- Do NOT let go of the thermometer while inserted in your cat.
- Do NOT attempt to take a temperature if your cat struggles.
- Do NOT take temperature by inserting the thermometer in the cat's mouth.

Taking a Pulse

The normal pulse rate is 150-240 beats per minute. There are 2 easy ways to take a pulse.

What to Do

Hand on Chest

- Grasp the chest just behind the elbows with one hand while supporting the cat with the other.

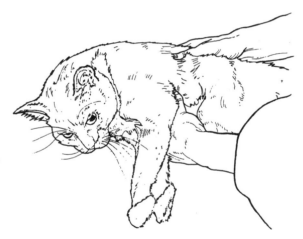

- Move the hand until you feel the heart beat.
- Count the number of beats in 20 seconds.
- Multiply that number by 3. For instance, 50 beats in 20 seconds would be 150 beats per minute.

Hand on the Femoral Artery

- Place fingers on inside of back leg where it joins the body.

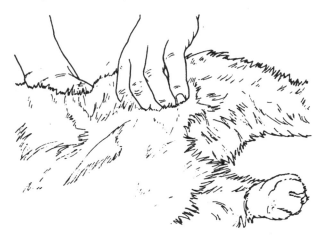

- Move fingers around until you feel the artery.
- Count the number of beats in 20 seconds.
- Multiply that number by 3. For instance, 60 beats in 20 seconds would be 180 beats per minute.

Taking a Respiratory Rate

The normal respiratory rate is between 10 and 30 breaths per minute. This rate can be much higher during and after play. The number of breaths per minute can be measured by watching the chest or by placing a tissue in front of the nose.

What to Do

Watch the Chest

- Watch how many times the cat breathes in 20 seconds (count only the number of times the cat fully inhales or fully exhales, not both).
- Multiply that number by 3. For instance, 8 breaths in 20 seconds is a rate of 24 per minute.

Using a Tissue

- Hold a tissue in front of the nose.

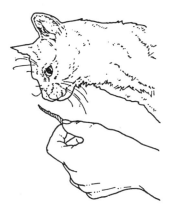

- Count how many times it moves in 20 seconds.
- Multiply that number by 3. For instance, if the tissue moves 6 times in 20 seconds, the rate is 18 per minute.

8. CPR: Life-Saving Procedures

Overview

CPR (cardiopulmonary resuscitation) consists of 2 procedures that may save the life of your cat: mouth-to-nose respiration and heart massage. While they may be life-saving, they can also be detrimental and you may aggravate your cat's condition if you do not properly administer these procedures.

You should not attempt either of these unless you encounter 2 conditions. Firstly, do not attempt CPR unless proper veterinary care is unavailable. If you can get to a veterinary surgeon quickly your cat will have a better chance of survival than if you try CPR yourself. Secondly, do not attempt either procedure unless it is obvious that your cat will die if you do nothing. In a horrible situation such as that, doing something is better than nothing at all.

If you attempt CPR and cannot revive your cat, do not think that you have failed. Trained professionals, using state-of-the-art techniques and drugs, often cannot save a cat. You can only do your best.

Mouth-to-Nose Respiration

After a serious accident your cat may stop breathing. If you cannot detect any signs of respiration and proper veterinary care is too far away you should try to get the lungs started again by giving mouth-to-nose respiration.

What to Do

- Clear the airway.
    - Open the mouth and pull the tongue forward.

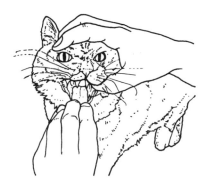

    - Remove any material that may be blocking the throat.
- Close mouth firmly.

- Place your mouth over the nose of the cat.

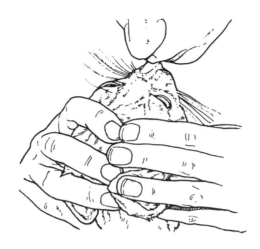

- Blow into nose until the chest expands fully (usually 1/2 to 1 second).
- Remove mouth from nose to allow the cat to exhale.
- Repeat the procedure for 10 seconds.
- Check to see if cat is breathing on its own. If not, repeat (several times if necessary).
- Transport to your veterinary surgeon as quickly as possible (see page **130**).

Heart Massage

After a serious accident the heart may stop beating. If there is no pulse and proper veterinary care is too far away, you should attempt to massage the heart.

What to Do

- Lay the cat on its side.
- Put one hand on the back along the spine.

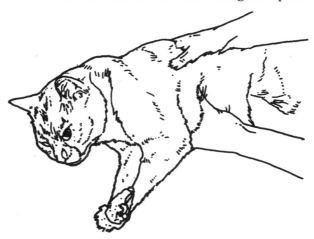

- Grasp the chest with the other hand.
- Push in firmly but gently (too much force may break the ribs).
- Repeat rapidly for 15 seconds.
- Check for pulse.
- Repeat, if necessary.
- Transport to your veterinary surgeon as quickly as possible (see page **130**).

CPR (Cardiopulmonary Resuscitation)

CPR is the combination of giving mouth-to-nose respiration and massaging the heart.

What to Do — One Person

- Do mouth-to-nose repiration for 10 seconds.
- Massage heart for 15 seconds.

- Check for breathing and a pulse rate.
- Repeat, if necessary.
- Transport to your veterinary surgeon as soon as possible (see page **130**).

What to Do — Two People

- One person gives mouth-to-nose respiration (usually ratio of 1 blow to 5 cardiac pumps).

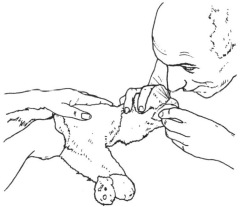

- The other person massages the heart.
- Continue for 10-15 seconds.
- Check for breathing and a pulse rate.
- Repeat, if necessary.
- Transport to your veterinary surgeon as soon as possible (see page **130**).

Crucial Points to Remember

Do NOT attempt mouth-to-nose respiration, heart massage or CPR unless. . .

- Proper veterinary care is not available.
- It is obvious that your cat will not survive if you do nothing.

9. The Unidentified Emergency

Overview

It is possible that you might encounter an emergency situation in which you have no idea as to what might be wrong or what caused the problem. In an instance such as this, you should transport your cat to your veterinary surgeon as quickly as possible. Your vet will probably ask you numerous questions while examining your pet. You should try to provide as much information as possible.

Signs of an Unidentified Emergency

- Cat collapsed or prostrate
- Unattributed unusual behaviour

What to Do

- Transport to your veterinary surgeon (see page **130**). While en route to the clinic, think back over the recent past. By reviewing your cat system by system, you might pick up some clues.

Questions you Should Ask yourself

General Questions
- Less alert than normal?
- Less active than normal?

- A change in appetite or drinking pattern?
- Outside for unusual period of time?
- Access to substances that may be poisonous, such as insecticides, antifreeze, medicines or mouse/rat poison?
- How long has there been a problem?

Respiratory System
- Difficulty breathing?
- Coughing or wheezing?
- Discharge from nose?
- Rapid respiratory rate?

Gastrointestinal System
- Vomiting or diarrhoea?
- Change in diet?
- Eating things that it should not?
- Bleeding from mouth or gums?
- Broken teeth?

Cardiovascular System
- Reduced tolerance to exercise?
- Change in colour of gums?

Urogenital System
- Straining to urinate?
- Urinating more frequently?
- Discharge from vulva or penis?

Neurological System
- Change in behaviour?
- Bumping into objects?
- Staring into space?
- Unstable posture or falling over?

Musculoskeletal System
- Limping?
- Pain if touched in certain areas?
- Difficulty in climbing stairs?
- Difficulty in standing up after lying for a period of time?

Skin
- Cuts or bruises?
- Bleeding?
- Hair loss?
- Excessive scratching?
- Biting at certain areas?
- Dull coat?
- Dirt or unusual substance on coat?
- Split or broken toenails?

Eyes
- Sensitivity to light?
- Discharge from eyes?
- Third eyelid across?

What NOT to Do

- Do NOT waste time in attempting to diagnose your cat's condition. An unidentified emergency is often very serious. The key to survival may be in obtaining proper medical evaluation and treatment as fast as possible.

10. Road Traffic Accidents, Falls and Trauma

Overview

The two most common causes of trauma for a cat are road traffic accidents and falling out of a window (the high-rise syndrome). This often results in very serious injuries such as a crushed chest, broken bones, brain concussions, open and closed wounds, internal bleeding and internal organ damage. In addition, the cat usually goes into shock.

Use care when handling an injured animal. A cat in pain may resist any manipulation and can inflict considerable damage. Should you be scratched or bitten by a cat, seek medical attention immediately.

You may not see your cat get hit by a car or fall from a great height, but you may suspect it if you notice several signs.

Signs of Road Traffic Accidents, Falls and Trauma

- Difficulty breathing
- Scrapes and cuts
- Pain
- Limping or dragging a leg
- Cannot stand up properly

- Bleeding from the nose
- Broken teeth or jaw
- Bruises
- Split toenails

What to Do — the ABCs

A good sequence of steps for first aid is known as the ABCs.

   A — Airway
   B — Breathing
   C — Circulation

If your cat shows no signs of life, transport to your veterinary surgeon immediately (see page 130). If proper medical care is unavailable, attempt CPR (see page 67).

Airway

Airway first aid involves clearing the airway so that the cat can breathe.

What To Do

- Pull the tongue out.

- Remove any blood or damaged tissue from the back of the mouth.

Breathing

Breathing first aid is ensuring that the cat is breathing properly.

If the cat is breathing, go to steps for Circulation (see page 80).

If there is a wound penetrating the chest cavity, air can enter the chest around the lungs. This makes normal breathing difficult or impossible. You should try to make an airtight seal over the wound.

Sign of Air Entering through a Wound

- Sucking noise as air goes in and out

What to Do

• Place cloth or plastic over the wound.

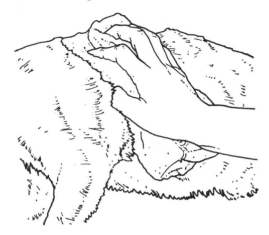

• Apply pressure until the noise stops.
• Hold in place with your hand or with tape.

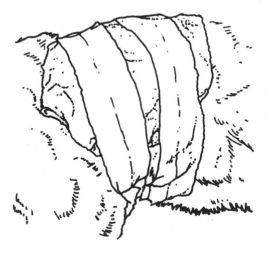

- Do NOT hold or apply the tape too tightly. This may make breathing even more difficult.
- Do NOT pull out objects from a chest wound.

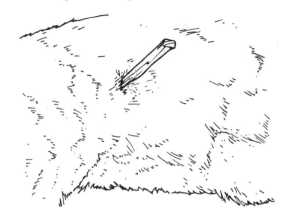

This may cause more damage. Place a bandage or plastic around any object sticking out of the chest.

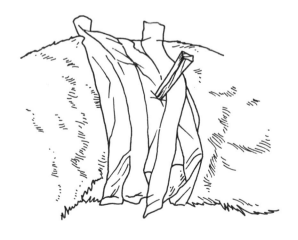

If the chest has been crushed, the cat will have difficulty breathing.

Signs of a Crushed Chest

- Standing with the elbows sticking out
- Using the abdomen to breathe
- Stretching out the neck

What to Do

- Try to find out which side of the chest is damaged the least.
- Lay the cat on its side with the least damaged side uppermost.
- Raise the head. (This helps clear the airway.)

Circulation

Circulation first aid involves controlling any bleeding.

Control bleeding by applying pressure.

What to Do

- Wad up some cloth or gauze.
- Place it directly over the wound.

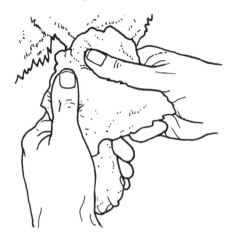

- Hold firmly but gently.

After the ABCs

What to Do

- Transport to your veterinary surgeon (see page **130**).

What NOT to Do

- Do NOT assume that your cat is out of danger if it appears to be unharmed. It may have suffered internal damage. The full extent of the injury may not be apparent for several hours or even days. By then, your cat may be in a critical condition.

11. Broken Legs, Sprains, Strains and Dislocations

Overview

Most broken bones (fractures) are caused by road traffic accidents or falling from heights. Fractures can be divided into 2 main groups: open and closed. An open fracture is when a bone breaks and cuts through the skin; it can easily become infected. If the skin is not pierced, it is a closed fracture. A major goal of closed fracture first aid is to prevent it from becoming an open fracture.

A sprain is a condition in which joints and ligaments twist beyond normal limits. A strain is the excessive stretching of muscles and tendons. A bone popping out of a joint or socket is a dislocation. It is difficult to tell the difference between a closed fracture and a sprain, strain or dislocation. Thus, they should be handled in a similar manner until veterinary care is obtained.

Use care when handling an injured animal. A cat in pain may resist any manipulation and can inflict considerable damage. If you are scratched or bitten by a cat, seek medical attention.

Signs of Breaks, Sprains, Strains and Dislocations

- Cracking or breaking sound at moment of impact

- Change in size, shape or length of the leg which may rest at a strange angle
- Standing on only three legs, the injured leg hanging limp
- Swelling around the injured area
- Pain
- Broken bone may be visible

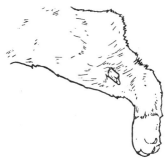

What to Do

- Move the injured leg as little as possible.
- If the bone is exposed, cover it with light gauze or a bandage. If this is too painful, covering the wound with a clean towel will help reduce contamination.

- Keep the cat as warm as possible; cover it with a blanket. This will reduce the effects of shock.
- Place a folded towel under the leg for support.

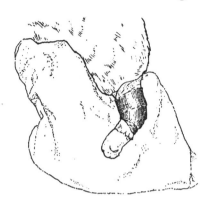

- Transport to your veterinary surgeon (see page **130**).

What NOT to Do

- Do NOT attempt to splint the leg. The swelling makes it difficult to determine the exact location of the injury. A cat in pain will probably resist manipulation of the injured limb. Forced treatment is painful and may cause more damage. Use a folded towel to support the leg.

12. Wounds

Overview

A wound is a break in the continuity of tissue in any part of the body. Frequently, it is painful. You must exercise caution when handling a wounded animal. A cat in pain may bite or lash out. If you are bitten or scratched, seek medical attention.

There are two basic types of wounds: closed and open. With most wounds there is a danger of infection. In addition, special steps should be taken if the wound is the result of a snake bite or insect sting.

Closed Wounds

A closed wound can be an abrasion or contusion (also known as a bruise); it is a wound where the skin remains unbroken. However, there may be significant internal damage that goes undetected. The injured skin may die and fall off a few days after the injury occurred; it may also become infected. The area affected is not always obvious and the extent of the damage may not be apparent for several days. A common cause of a closed wound is heavy friction on the skin or a blow from a blunt object.

Signs of a Closed Wound

- Pain

- Heat in a small area
- Skin appears scratched
- Swelling

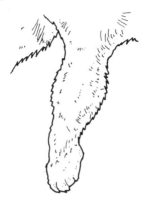

What to Do

- Bathe the area in cold water.
- Apply an ice pack. Use an icebag or place ice in a towel.

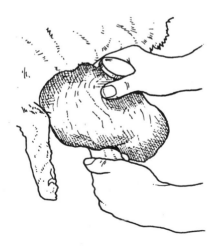

- If the skin is scratched up, clean with 3% hydrogen peroxide or salt water (1 teaspoon of salt to half a litre of warm water).
- Transport to your veterinary surgeon (see page **130**). If the wound appears serious, go to your vet immediately. If not, go as soon as possible. All minor wounds should be checked by a vet within 24 hours.

What NOT to Do

- Do NOT underestimate a closed wound. While it may look harmless, it can hide major internal damage. The full extent of the damage may not be apparent for several days. By then, your cat's condition may be very serious.

Open Wounds

An open wound is where the skin is broken, usually accompanied by significant bleeding. The loss of large amounts of blood can be life threatening. In addition, muscles, tendons, blood vessels and nerves may be severed and internal organs may be damaged. Dirt and bacteria can enter the wound, leading to possible infection.

Signs of an Open Wound

- Pain
- Limping

- Excessive licking of certain areas
- Bleeding

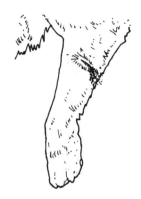

What to Do

- Use pressure to control the bleeding.
    - Wad up some clean cloth or gauze.
    - Place directly over the wound.
    - Hold firmly but gently.

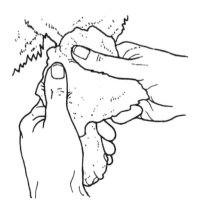

- If the wound is minor, clean the wound.
  - Flush the wound with 3% hydrogen peroxide or salt water (1 teaspoon of salt to half a litre of warm water).

  - Gently clean the wound with gauze or cloth. Do NOT rub. This hurts and may cause more damage.

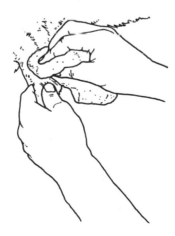

- Transport to your veterinary surgeon (see page **130**). A cat with a major wound should go to the vet immediately. A minor wound should be checked within 24 hours.

What NOT to Do

- Do NOT delay transporting to your veterinary surgeon. Use pressure to control the bleeding while en route.
- Do NOT pull out an object that has penetrated a body cavity such as the chest or abdomen. This might cause more damage.

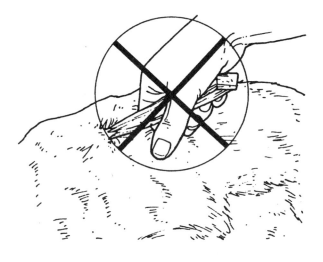

- Do NOT underestimate a small open wound. The cut may be deep and susceptible to infection.

Infection

Infection can be a complication of any wound. It involves the growth of bacteria leading to heat, redness, swelling and pain. An infected limb may be so swollen and painful that it may resemble a broken leg. Infection can spread into the bloodstream, usually causing the cat to run a fever and to go off its food. A very serious infection can end in major surgery or possibly death. A common result of a cat bite is an abscess. Likely areas for an abscess are the head, legs and base of the tail.

Signs of Infection

- Swelling
- Limping
- Pain
- Coloured discharge – may be cream, yellow, green, brown or blood-tinged
- Foul odour

What to Do

- Transport to your veterinary surgeon (see page **130**).

Snake Bites

Most snakes are not poisonous. However, all of the species of viper in Europe are. A viper has 2 fangs that puncture the skin and pump the venom.

The parts of a cat usually bitten are the head and the legs. If you cannot identify the snake when the cat is bitten and the wound consists of 2 small openings close together, assume that the snake is poisonous.

A cat bitten by a poisonous snake is in a very serious predicament. The 2 keys to survival are keeping the cat quiet and obtaining prompt medical attention. Fortunately in the UK it is rare for cats to be bitten by vipers.

Signs of a Snake Bite

- Two deep punctures

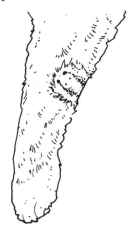

- Swelling
- Area tender and painful to touch
- Weakness
- Wobbling
- Acting nervously

What to Do

- Identify the type of snake, if possible.
- Keep animal quiet.
- Restrict its movement. This reduces the amount of venom pumped around the body.
- Apply a tourniquet only if the bite is on the lower part of a leg and you think that the snake was poisonous.
  - Wrap a thin belt, bandage or string several times around the leg above the wound.

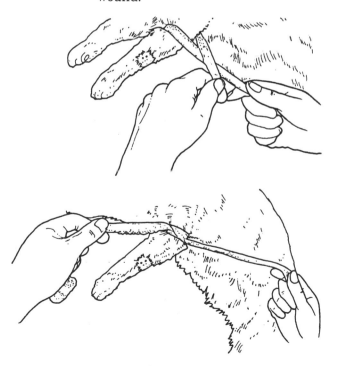

• Tie into a bow.

• The tourniquet should be snug but not too tight. You should be able to slip a finger under the tourniquet. The goal is to restrict the flow of blood, not to stop it.

• Keep the cat warm. This reduces the effect of shock.

- Transport to your veterinary surgeon (see page **130**). If you cannot reach medical attention within a short period of time, loosen the tourniquet for 60 seconds every 10 minutes.

What NOT to Do

- Do NOT cut the wound and try to suck out the snake venom. This rarely helps and may cause more damage.
- Do NOT apply a tourniquet if the cat resists. Exciting the cat will hasten the spread of the toxins around the body. Place an ice-pack, if available, over the bite. This will also reduce the bloodflow and therefore the spread of the venom.

Insect Stings

Most insect stings are painful but harmless. However, it is possible that a cat may have an allergic reaction to the insect venom, causing its airway passages to contract. This makes breathing difficult and reduces the effectiveness of the cardiovascular system. The end result can be shock and sometimes death.

Signs of an Insect Sting

- Swelling, usually around the face or legs
- Heat felt when touched
- Possible shock within 30 minutes (if an allergic reaction takes place)

What to Do

- Remove stinger if still in cat.
    - Use tweezers.
    - Grasp stinger at point of entry into the skin.

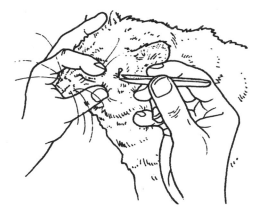

    - Pull straight out using a steady, even pressure.
- Apply a cold compress or cloth soaked in cold water.
- Transport to your veterinary surgeon (see page **130**).

What NOT to Do

- When removing a stinger, do NOT squeeze the venom sack. This will inject more venom into the cat.

13. Feline Urological Syndrome (FUS) and the 'Blocked' Cat

Overview

Feline urological syndrome (FUS) is the common term for lower urinary tract disease. It can be caused by the formation of sand, stones or mucous plugs, urethral infection, bladder infection, cancer of the urethra or bladder, metabolic disorders, congenital abnormalities or any combination of these problems. Cats suffering from FUS usually experience pain or irritation when urinating.

Untreated, FUS can lead to a 'blocked' cat. This occurs when mucous plugs, sand, grit or small stones (known as calculi) block the urethra and prevent the passage of urine from the bladder. As a result, the bladder backs up and diminishes the kidney's ability to function as the body's filter. This leads to a build up of toxic by-products in the body. The end result is that the cat is poisoned. This problem most commonly appears in young males; females are very rarely blocked. A blocked cat cannot pass urine, can be in a great deal of pain and will often go off its food and water. It is a life-threatening situation that requires immediate medical attention.

The risk of FUS and blockage can be reduced by feeding your cat a special diet that contains a urinary acidifier and is restricted in certain minerals. The low mineral content reduces the amount of minerals excreted in the urine. The acidifier helps keep the minerals that are excreted in a soluble form. The combination of the 2 help prevent the formation of sand, grit and stones.

Signs of FUS

- Frequent urination with small amounts of urine being passed
- Licking at the genitalia
- Blood in urine
- Unusual behaviour (such as urinating in uncommon areas of house)
- May eat less than normal

What to Do

- Transport to your veterinary surgeon immediately if the cat is a male (see page **130**). If the cat is definitely a female and not in obvious discomfort, transport to your vet within 24 hours.

Signs of a 'Blocked' Cat (almost always a Male)

- Frequent crouching and straining to urinate with little or no passing of urine
- May appear to be constipated
- Penis sticking out, usually dry and purple in colour
- Licking at genitalia

- May cry in pain when picked up
- Lethargic
- Not eating
- Vomiting
- Change in behaviour; may be scared and/or vicious

What to Do

- Transport to your veterinary surgeon immediately (see page **130**). The length of time between blockage and treatment may determine the extent of kidney damage. Serious damage can be fatal.

14. Burns

Overview

A burn is the destruction of tissue by extreme localized heat. The severity of a burn is measured by the depth of skin affected and how much surface area is covered. Often the full extent of a burn is not known until several days after the accident.

There are 3 types of burns.

- Thermal burns
- Chemical burns
- Electrical burns

A thermal burn is the most common. It is caused by being scalded by boiling water, touching an open flame or coming in contact with a hot surface such as an oven door or stove-top. A thermal burn will turn the skin red and may cause blistering. The hair around the burn may be singed.

A chemical burn is caused by spillage of a corrosive material on the cat. A substance containing an alkali such as lye or ammonia will turn the affected area white or brown and will give the skin a soapy or slippery feel. An acidic substance will cause the skin to dehydrate, contract and darken. Acid burns are very painful, unless the nerve endings have been killed. This would result in no pain but is still very serious.

An electrical burn is discussed in Chapter 15 (see page **104**).

Signs of Burns

- Skin turning red, white or brown
- Hair singed or falling out in spots

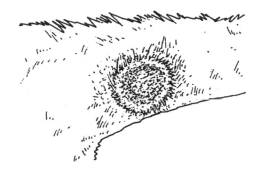

- Skin painful to touch
- Skin contracting
- Skin soapy or slippery to feel
- Blisters

What to Do

- Put on rubber gloves, if available. If you do not wear gloves while treating a chemical burn, you may also be burned.
- Clean and treat burn.

For Burns that Leave the Skin Intact
• Wash burned area with cold water. Use
  a gentle stream or place in a bath

• Put a cold compress on the area burned
  (The faster the skin is cooled down, the
  less damage will occur and the greater
  the chance for a favourable outcome)

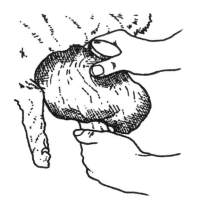

For Burns that Go through the Entire Thickness of the Skin.
- Cover with a dry cloth or towel (Washing the burn is too painful)

- Transport to your veterinary surgeon (see page **130**).

What NOT to Do

- Do NOT underestimate a burn. It is prone to infection and is easily complicated. A burn covering as little as 15% of the body can be life-threatening.
- Do NOT put oils or creams on the burn. Substances such as butter or margarine do not help.

15. Electrocution

Overview

Electrocution occurs when an electrical current passes through the body. It commonly happens when a cat chews through an electrical cord. It can also be caused by contact with power lines, touching exposed wires and being struck by lightning.

There are 2 problems caused by electrocution. Firstly, the electrical current can create tremendous heat and cause an electrical burn. Secondly, the current may result in the shut down of key organs such as the heart, the lungs and the kidneys.

The danger of electrocution is deceptive. An animal may appear to recover from a shock within a few minutes. However, the full effects may not appear until 24 to 48 hours after the event. Possible consequences are that the lungs gradually fill with fluid or that the heart may develop an abnormal rhythm. Any cat that has been electrocuted should be examined by a veterinary surgeon.

Preventing Electrocution

Since most cases of electrocution occur by chewing through electrical cords, kittens that are teething or going through a chewing phase are especially at risk. You can take a few steps to minimize the chance of an accident.

- Unplug cords and equipment not in use
- Replace old or frayed wires
- Use a product designed to deter chewing. This is applied directly to an object and has a bitter taste that most cats do not like

Signs of Electrocution

- Burns, usually around the mouth (most burns will have a pale center surrounded by redness and swelling)
- Convulsions
- Collapsed or lying on side
- Low respiratory rate (under 10 breaths per minute)
- Loss of consciousness
- Heart may have stopped
- Voiding urine and faeces

What to Do

- Switch off electrical source.
- Check for vital signs. Is the cat breathing and does it have a heartbeat?
- Transport to your veterinary surgeon (see page **130**). If vital signs are absent and proper veterinary care is not available, attempt CPR (see page **67**). Even if your cat appears to fully recover, you should contact your vet immediately.

What NOT to Do

* Do NOT touch the cat if it is still in contact with the electrical current. If you do, you may also be electrocuted. If the cat is touching the source of electricity and is very rigid, it is probably still being shocked. Also watch for any water that may be in contact with the cat.

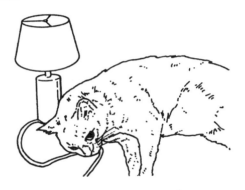

* Before touching the cat, turn off the electricity by shutting it off at the source or pulling out the plug (**do not touch any exposed wires**). If you cannot shut off the electricity, move the cat with a non-metal object, such as a broomstick.

16. Heat Stroke

Overview

The cat uses its respiratory system to control its body temperature. When hot, cats inhale cool air through the nose and exhale hot air through the mouth. The faster cats breathe, the quicker their bodies cool down.

This process works as long as the outside temperature is under the normal 38.3-39°C (101-102°F) body temperature of cats. When the outside temperature approaches or exceeds this, a cat cannot efficiently cool itself down. The inability to lose excess body heat can result in heat stroke. This causes a reduction of blood circulation, reduced performance of the kidneys (the blood cleaning filter) and swelling of the brain. It has a high mortality rate.

The most common cases of heat stroke result from leaving cats in cars. On a hot day, the temperature in a car can reach 55°C (130°F) in a short period of time. The temperature can soar even if the windows are open. Keeping a cat in a room without good ventilation can also cause heat stroke. Accidentally trapping a cat in a clothes dryer is a third cause. If a dryer is warm and the door is open, a cat may crawl in for a nap. You can then inadvertently shut the door and start the machine with the cat inside.

The chance of heat stroke can be diminished simply

by not leaving a cat in a car during the summer, by keeping a fan on low when it is confined to the home and by checking the clothes dryer before starting it.

Signs of Heat Stroke

- Extreme panting
- Excessive salivation
- Collapse
- Anxious expression on face
- Rectal temperature of 40.5°C (105°F) or higher

What to Do

- Get the cat's temperature down.
  - immerse in (or hose down with) cold water. Keep in water until the temperature goes down.

- Or give an alcohol bath.
  - Soak the legs with rubbing alcohol.

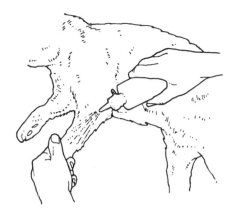

• Pour a small amount on the body.

• Place an ice pack on the head and around the body.
• Check the body temperature with a rectal thermometer every 5 minutes. Stop heat reduction when the temperature reaches 39.5°C (103°F). Do not be alarmed if the temperature drops a few degrees below normal. A high temperature is much more

serious than a low one.

- Give cold water to drink. Allow to drink as much as possible.
- Vigorously massage the legs. This helps maintain the blood flow and counteracts shock.

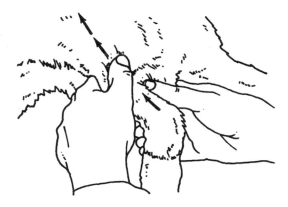

- Transport to your veterinary surgeon (see page **130**). The cat should be examined even if its temperature drops back to normal quickly.

What NOT to Do

- Do NOT put the cat's head under water when immersing it.
- Do NOT put alcohol on the cat's head when giving an alcohol bath.

17. Cold Exposure and Frostbite

Overview

Cold exposure (also known as hypothermia) happens when the body temperature becomes much lower than the normal range of 38.3-39°C (101-102°F). All cats are at risk because of their large body surface relative to their body weight, which facilitates heat loss. Kittens, older cats and injured cats are especially vulnerable. Exposure is very serious and frequently results in death.

In addition, exposure to cold may cause frostbite, a condition in which the skin tissue begins to die. It is possible to develop this condition without suffering serious hypothermia. The parts of a cat prone to frostbite are the tail, tips of the ears and footpads. Frostbitten tissue is very fragile and should be handled very carefully.

The chance of cold exposure and frostbite can be greatly diminished if the cat is brought inside when the temperature falls below freezing or in extreme cold, windy weather.

Signs of Cold Exposure

- Stiff muscles
- Shivering

- Cold to touch
- Dilated and fixed eye pupils
- Low pulse rate (below 150 beats per minute)
- Low respiratory rate (below 10 breaths per minute)
- Body temperature below 38.3°C (101°F)

Signs of Frostbite

- Scaling of the skin
- Loss of hair
- White hair
- A leathery feel to the skin

What to Do

- Handle carefully and very gently.
- Warm cat slowly.
    - Wrap in a blanket.
    - A hot water bottle can be used. Place it underneath the blanket, not directly in contact with the cat.

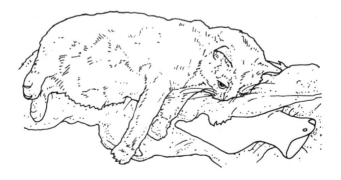

- A hair dryer can be used. Set on warm, not hot.
- Transport to your veterinary surgeon (see page **130**). If you cannot reach medical attention quickly, place the cat in a sink or tub of warm water (40-43°C [104-109°F]). Keep its head above water.

What NOT to Do

- Do NOT warm cat too quickly. Because the blood supply to the skin and limbs has been shut down, hypothermic cats can easily be burned.

18. Choking and Object in the Mouth

Overview

Choking occurs when an animal cannot breathe normally due to an object in its throat blocking the airway. Kittens are especially at risk because they often try to swallow the objects that they chew on while teething. These objects can become stuck in the throat causing the animal to choke. If your cat is choking, you must immediately attempt to dislodge the object blocking the airway; do not wait for veterinary assistance. Choking can be fatal.

It is possible that an object can be stuck in the mouth without causing the animal to choke. While the cat may be able to breathe, the object may shift and subsequently block the airway. Therefore, it is potentially dangerous and should be removed as quickly as possible.

Use care when handling an injured animal. A cat that is choking or has an object stuck in its mouth may panic and can inflict considerable damage. It may lash out or try to bite you when you attempt to remove the object. If you are injured, seek medical attention.

Signs of Choking

- Not able to breathe

- Rubbing face on ground
- Pawing at mouth
- Eyes bulging
- Blue tongue
- Choking sound

What to Do

- Try to remove the object by hand.
  - Hold cat securely. A good method is to wrap it in a thick towel with only the head sticking out.

  - Open mouth wide.
  - Grab object with hand.
  - Pull out gently.

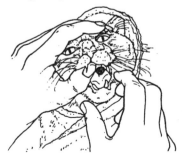

- If unsuccessful, pick up by back legs. Swing back and forth several times.

- If unsuccessful, use the Heimlich manoeuvre. This forces air out of the lungs and blows the object out of the airway.
  - Lay cat on side.
  - Place one hand on spine behind the chest.
  - Grasp the lower part of the rib cage with the other hand.

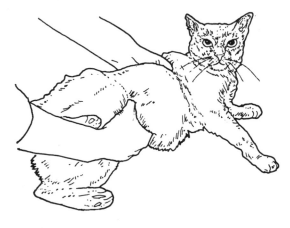

- Using hand on the lower ribs, squeeze in and upward. This action forces air out of lungs and should blow the object out of the throat (too much force may cause internal damage).
- If object is still stuck, repeat rapidly several times.
- Transport to your veterinary surgeon (see page **130**). If that is not possible, and the cat has no pulse or respiratory rates, attempt CPR (see page **67**).

What NOT to Do

- Do NOT wait for a veterinary surgeon to remove the object blocking the airway. A choking cat cannot breathe and will probably die within a short period of time. You must take action.
- Do NOT assume that the crisis is over when the object is removed. The throat will often swell up when something has been stuck in it. This swelling might block the airway. In addition, internal damage may have occurred by use of the Heimlich manoeuvre. The cat should be examined by your vet as soon as possible.

Signs of Having an Object in the Mouth

- Excessive drooling
- Rubbing face on ground
- Pawing at mouth
- Difficulty in swallowing
- Interest in food, but not eating

What to Do

- Try to remove the object by hand. Use the same procedure as with choking (see page **115**).
- Transport to your veterinary surgeon (see page **130**).

What NOT to Do

- Do NOT force the removal of the object by hand. If it does not come out easily, leave it in place and transport to your vet immediately.
- Do NOT pull out string or thread if part of it has been swallowed. It might saw through the stomach or intestines.
- Do NOT pull out fish hooks or any objects embedded in tissue. This might cause more damage and serious bleeding.
- Do NOT struggle with your cat. If it is uncooperative, take it to your veterinary surgeon.

19. Poisons

Overview

A poison is any substance that can cause illness or death if it gets into the body. Most animal poisonings are caused by ingestion, inhalation, absorption or injection. Two of the most common ways are eating a poisonous house plant and licking off excess flea and tick medicine from the skin.

There are thousands of poisonous substances. As a result, the large variety of symptoms makes diagnosis difficult. Frequently, a veterinary surgeon has to attempt treatment when the type of poison is not known or when it is not certain that the animal has been poisoned. It is important to convey as much information as possible to your vet.

Generally, you will not see your cat poison itself. You might assume this has happened if your cat is acting in a peculiar manner (especially if it has been missing for a period of time).

If you see your cat eat or come in contact with a poison, take it to your veterinary surgeon immediately. Do not wait until signs of toxicity develop.

Poison Prevention

Many cases of poisoning are caused by cats eating something that is around the house. There are several steps that can be taken to prevent this from happening.

- Make a list of all plants in the home and garden
    - Find out which are poisonous
    - Remove them or keep them out of reach
- Never give medication intended for humans, such as aspirin or other pain-relieving products, to your cat unless instructed to do so by your vet
- Keep all chemicals, cleaning fluids, insecticides, fertilizers and medicines out of reach. Other common household poisons are antifreeze and mouse, rat, cockroach and slug poison
- Do not overuse medical compounds such as flea and tick products. Always read and follow the instructions carefully

Signs of Poisoning

- Severe vomiting
- Severe diarrhoea
- Shaking
- Convulsions
- Blood in vomit, faeces or urine
- Bluish colour to tongue
- Weakness
- Collapse
- Difficulty breathing
- Excessive drooling
- Severe irritation of the eyes or mouth
- Peculiar substance on skin or coat

What to Do

- If the poison is on the skin, wash the substance off.

- Use a lot of water.
- Wear rubber gloves to avoid contaminating yourself.
- Allow cat to drink as much water as possible – water dilutes most poisons.
- Give activated charcoal tablets, if available – charcoal absorbs many poisons.
- Get a sample of the poison, if possible.
- Get a sample of vomit or stool, if the poison is not available.
- Transport to your veterinary surgeon (see page **130**). Telephone before departing. Your vet may give special instructions to induce vomiting to limit absorption.

What NOT to Do

- Do NOT wait for signs of poisoning to develop. Take your cat to your veterinary surgeon if you see it ingest or come into contact with a toxic substance.
- Do NOT induce vomiting unless directed to do so by your vet. Many poisons will burn the throat.
- Do NOT give anything by mouth if the cat is convulsing or unconscious.
- Do NOT give any medication especially aspirin or other pain-relieving products unless directed to do so by your veterinary surgeon. Most common pain killers are highly toxic to cats.

20. Vomiting and Diarrhoea

Overview

There are a large number of causes of vomiting and diarrhoea, the effects of which range from insignificant to extremely serious. Examples include intestinal parasites, bacterial infections, motion sickness, internal foreign bodies, kidney failure and poisoning. Since the list is virtually endless, professional help is essential to distinguish between the different causes. The most common cause is a sudden change of diet. A cat, accustomed to the effects of a particular food, may suffer an upset stomach if the diet is abruptly changed. With a kitten, any vomiting or diarrhoea should be considered potentially serious.

Prevention of Vomiting and Diarrhoea

There are a few steps that you can take to eliminate many of the common causes.

- Treat your cat for worms every 3 months
- Do NOT feed your cat table scraps
- Avoid changing the type of food suddenly
- Do NOT allow your cat to nibble on house plants
- Groom your cat everyday to reduce the chance of hairballs
- Limit access to items that can be swallowed, such as string, yarn and thread

Signs — Not Serious

- Vomiting/diarrhoea occurs only once or twice
- No other problems

What to Do

- Withhold all food for 24 hours.
- Give water.
- If symptoms stop after 24 hours, feed boiled white meat off the bone (chicken, turkey or white fish) with boiled white rice for 2 to 3 days. Gradually switch back to regular food.

Signs — Serious

- Symptoms lasting more than 24 hours
- Frequent vomiting or diarrhoea
- Blood in stool or vomit
- Fever
- Evidence of pain
- Weakness or collapse
- Dehydration (eyes sunk in sockets and skin not springing back into place when pinched)
- Signs of other problems (like runny eyes or nose and high respiratory rate)
- Any vomiting and diarrhoea by a kitten

What to Do

- Transport to your veterinary surgeon (see page **130**).

21. Drowning

Overview

Drowning occurs when the lungs of an animal become flooded with fluid. This stops the inhalation of air and shuts down the respiratory system. Even if a drowning episode does not stop the animal from breathing, it can be serious. Excess fluid can damage the lungs, reducing their ability to absorb oxygen. As a result, a life-threatening situation may exist several hours after the incident occurred.

Drowning is uncommon among cats because they are naturally wary of water. In addition, most are good swimmers over short distances.

Signs of Drowning

- Panic and frantic effort to swim
- Motionless in water

What to Do

- Pull tongue out of mouth.

- Drain the water from the lungs.
  - Pick up by hind legs.

  - Gently swing back and forth until fluid stops coming out.
- Transport to your veterinary surgeon (see page **130**). If this is not possible and the cat has no pulse or respiratory rates, attempt CPR (see page **67**).

What NOT to Do

- Do NOT assume that the emergency is over if the cat appears to recover. Internal damage to the lungs may have occurred and might lead to secondary flooding over a period of several hours. Such damage may limit the ability of the lungs to function properly, reducing the amount of oxygen absorbed into the bloodstream.

22. Seizures

Overview

A seizure, also known as a fit, occurs when a cat appears to lose control of its body due to a malfunction of the brain. In controlling the nervous system, the brain acts like a computer. It stores a massive amount of information and sends messages to the various parts of the body via electrical impulses. When a seizure occurs, the impulses that excite or turn on a body function may overwhelm those that suppress or turn off a function. This produces uncontrollable twitching and erratic behaviour. The most common cause of seizures is epilepsy. However, seizures can be the result of several other afflictions such as tumours, hyperthyroidism, meningitis or poisoning.

There are 2 types of seizure. A generalized seizure (or grand mal seizure) affects the entire brain. A partial seizure (also known as a focal seizure or petit mal seizure), only affects a portion of the brain. However, it can grow to become a generalized seizure.

For cats that suffer recurring seizures, medication may be prescribed. These drugs do not always prevent seizures, but they may help reduce the number and severity. If your veterinary surgeon does prescribe medication, you should give it regularly. Failure to do so may bring on a seizure.

If your cat has seizures, you should keep a log book. It should record when a seizure takes place and how long it lasts. If you notice that the seizures are occurring more frequently or for longer periods of time, contact your veterinary surgeon within 24 hours.

Signs of a Generalized Seizure

- Lying on side
- Cycling movement of legs
- Rolling of eyes
- Frothing of mouth
- Moving jaw rapidly
- Voiding urine and faeces

Signs of a Partial Seizure

- Bumping into objects
- Standing and staring into space
- Trying to catch imaginary flies
- Localized twitching of muscles

What to Do

- Stop animal from hurting itself.

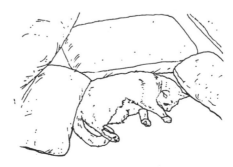

- Move it to a safe area away from furniture and stairwells
- Place blankets or pillows around it
- Time the length of the seizure

What NOT to Do

- Do NOT put your hand near the cat's mouth
- Do NOT give anything by mouth

After the Seizure

- Place cat in a dark room
- Keep quiet. Do not make any sudden movements or loud noises
- Give a moderate amount of food and water.
- Wipe away excess saliva
- Clean up urine and faeces
- Take rectal temperature, if possible

Contact your Veterinary Surgeon Immediately if. . .

- It is your cat's first seizure
- It has more than one seizure in a 24-hour period
- The seizure lasts more than 3 minutes and the cat does not recover quickly and completely. Long, continual seizures can cause death

- The rectal temperature is over 40°C (104°F)

Contact your Veterinary Surgeon within 24 Hours if. . .

- The cat is already on anti-seizure medication
- It has a single, short seizure lasting less than 3 minutes and recovers quickly and completely

23. Transporting your Cat to the Vet

Overview

Moving a critically injured animal is dangerous; even a slight movement can cause great damage. In addition, an animal in pain may lash out at you. It is crucial that you take precautions to reduce the chance of further injury and to protect both your pet and yourself. Seek medical attention if a cat does wound you.

Things to Remember

- **Support the Back:** a seriously injured cat may have a broken back. If the back is not evenly supported when the cat is picked up, a broken bone may pull apart or the ends of the break may rub. This may cut the spinal cord, paralysing the cat. The back can be supported by sliding a thick towel beneath the cat prior to lifting. If a towel cannot be used, try to keep the back straight when lifting the cat.

- **Keep a Broken Leg up:** if you suspect that the cat has a broken leg, place it on its side; the damaged limb should be uppermost. This keeps the weight of the body off the injured leg. You might give the limb some support by placing a folded blanket or towel underneath it.

- **Keep the Damaged Side of a Chest down:** if you suspect that the chest has been crushed, attempt to determine if one side of the chest is in better shape than the other. If this can be done, transport the cat with the least damaged side of the chest up. The lung on that side will function better than the one on the most damaged side. A cat lying with the most damaged side of the chest pointing up may have difficulty breathing. If there is both a broken leg and a crushed chest, the crushed chest should take priority.

Transporting a Cat with Minor Injuries

A cat with minor injuries should be handled in a normal manner. Placing it in a catbox will protect both the cat and you. Use special care not to aggravate the injury. Wrapping the cat in a towel can support an injured limb and help cover a wound. It will also help keep the animal warm, reducing the effects of shock.

Transporting a Cat with Critical Injuries

Most cats can be transported by one person. It is a good idea to slide a towel under the cat and then place both in a cat box. The towel will help support the back while the box will protect both the cat and you. However, do not waste time searching for a towel or a box if they are not readily available.

What to Do

• Position the cat to be picked up.

  • The back is toward you.
  • The side with a broken leg is uppermost.
    Place a towel or cloth under the leg for
    additional support.
  • The damaged side of the chest is down-
    most.

• Slide a folded towel under the cat.
• Slide hands beneath the towel under the
  cat's body.

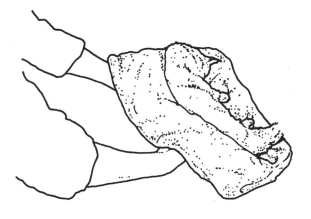

- Pick up using one continuous, fluid motion. Support the back with your hands and forearm.

- Place in catbox.

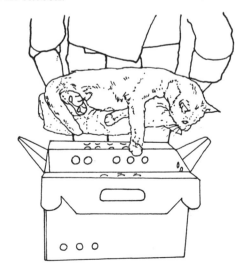

- Walk carefully and smoothly to the car

- Place the cat on seat or in the front foot-well on the floor, with its back towards the rear of the car. Position so that the cat or catbox does not shoot forwards if the driver brakes suddenly
- Keep warm to reduce the effect of shock.
    - Place a blanket over the cat
    - Turn on the heater in the car
- Drive carefully to your veterinary clinic

What NOT to Do

- Do NOT make any sudden movements. The goals are to move the cat as little as possible and to move it smoothly when you must

PART III

AFTER THE EMERGENCY

24. Giving Medication

Overview

To complete the treatment of your cat, your veterinary surgeon may prescribe medication for you to administer. The medication serves no purpose if you do not give it in the right dosage at the right times. Your vet will instruct you on when and how to give medication.

Sometimes the prescribed drug will not have the desired effect. In cases such as this, another kind of drug or treatment may be recommended. However, it is impossible to determine the effectiveness of a medication if the instructions are not followed.

Some cats will not allow you to give them medication, despite your best efforts. Care must be taken to avoid being bitten or scratched by an uncooperative, angry animal. If you are injured, you should seek medical attention.

If you are having difficulty giving medicine, contact your veterinary surgeon. You might be advised to use an alternative method or to go to the clinic to have the medicine administered by injection.

Giving Pills

By Hand

- Place your cat on a raised surface so that it

cannot back up. A table next to a wall or someone holding the cat from behind, works well

- Open mouth
    - Place one hand on the cat's muzzle. The thumb is just behind one canine tooth, the index finger behind the other
    - Pull head back
    - Other hand pulls the jaw down

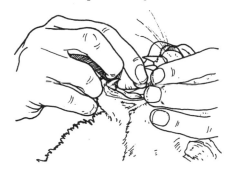

- Drop the pill as far back on the tongue as possible

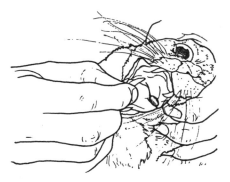

- Touch the pill quickly and gently with the tip of your finger
- Close mouth
- Rub the throat until the cat swallows

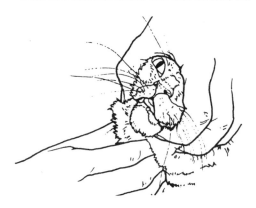

- Open mouth to check if the pill went down. If it did not, repeat

By Tricking the Cat

- Grind up the pill
- Mix it in with some food that your cat loves

Giving Liquid Medication

By Hand

- Open mouth
  - Place one hand on the cat's muzzle. The thumb is just behind one canine tooth, the index finger behind the other
  - Keep head level. Do not tilt back as for pills

- Other hand pulls the jaw down
- Squirt liquid into the side of the mouth. Do not squirt into the back. The liquid may go down the windpipe instead of the throat

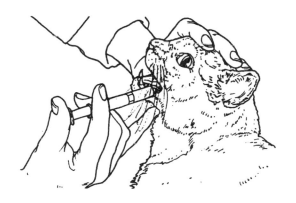

- Close mouth
- Rub the throat until the cat swallows
- Open mouth to check if the liquid went down. If not, repeat

By Tricking the Cat

- Fill a bowl with the cat's favourite food
- Mix the liquid in thoroughly

Medicating the Eyes

The common types of medication for the eyes are ointments and drops. It is important that these come into direct contact with the eyeball.

Ointment

- Clean away any discharge; use a tissue or cotton wool soaked in warm water
- Separate the lower eyelid from the eyeball
  - Hold the cat's head with one hand so that your index finger is on the upper eyelid and the thumb is on the lower eyelid

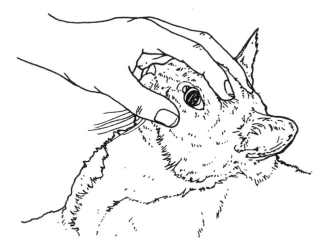

- Move the thumb downward while holding the index finger steady. This creates a small cup between the lower eyelid and the eye

- Rest the hand holding the tube of ointment on the side of the head

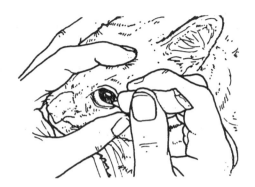

- Run a bead of ointment in the cup. (Use care not to touch the eye with the tube; it might scratch the cornea)
- Gently close the upper and lower eyelids together. This will cause the ointment to spread a thin film over the eyeball and socket. (Do not worry if the eye turns white; it should clear within a few minutes)

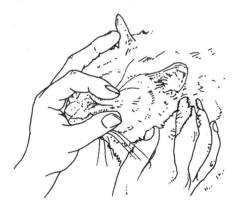

Drops

- Clean away any discharge; use a tissue or cotton wool soaked in warm water
- Gently tilt the head back
- Separate the upper eyelid from the eyeball.
    - Hold the cat's head with one hand so that your index finger is on the upper eyelid and the thumb is on the lower eyelid
    - Move the index finger upward while holding the thumb steady
- Rest the hand holding the eye dropper on the side of the head

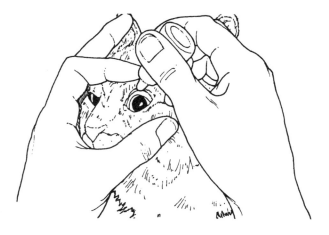

- Place the drops onto the upper portion of the eyeball. (Use care not to touch the eyeball with the dropper; it might scratch the cornea)

Medicating the Ears

The ear canal of a cat has 2 sections (the vertical and horizontal canals) with wax glands just in front of the eardrum. It is important that the medication traverses both sections and reaches the eardrum.

- Expose the ear canal by holding up the ear flap
- Place the ointment or drops in the ear canal

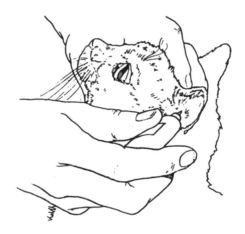

- Massage the ear canal by rubbing the back of the ear where it meets the head. You may hear a squelching sound. That means that the medicine is making its way down the canal to the eardrum. Massage for 2 minutes or for as long as possible

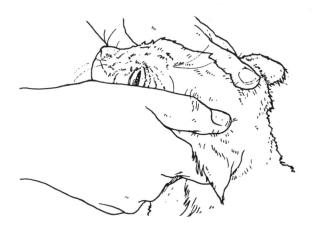

- Wipe away the excess fluid using your finger and a wad of cotton wool. Do not insert anything deep into the ear canal

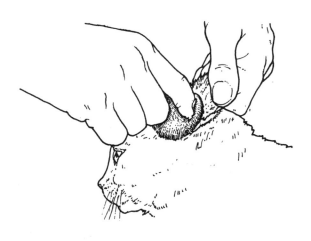

25. Splints, Bandages and Surgical Drains

Overview

Splints, bandages and surgical drains are important aids to healing. A splint holds a limb in the correct position so that it can mend. A bandage keeps a wound clean, helps to prevent infection and protects against further injury. A surgical drain is placed in a wound so that excess fluid does not collect. If one of these devices is being used, you should check it often. If you discover any swelling, excessive discharge, foul odours or additional sores, you should contact your veterinary surgeon.

When checking areas of your cat that may be painful, use care to avoid being bitten or scratched. Seek medical attention if you are wounded.

Splints

A splint is used to position a leg to facilitate the healing of broken bones. It has to be snug enough to hold the limb in the correct position. However, it should not be so tight that it restricts bloodflow, which leads to swelling or causes pressure sores. A splint is difficult to place; most cats need to be anaesthetized or sedated before one can be applied. Caring for one can also be difficult.

Care of a Splint

- Check top and bottom for swelling 3 times a day. Do this by putting your finger in both the top and bottom of the splint
  - The top of the splint should be snug but you should be able to insert your finger

  - If the toes are exposed you should be able to put your finger between them. They should not be cold or swollen

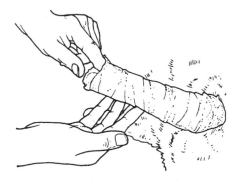

- Check for rubbing and sores 3 times a day
  - The top of the splint should be able to move slightly when the leg is moved
  - Your finger should be dry when you pull it out from between the toes if they are exposed. If it is not, there may be open sores draining fluid
- Keep the splint clean. Put an old sock over it and tape it in place
- Keep the cat quiet. It is best kept indoors throughout the convalescent period
- If it chews the splint, put an Elizabethan collar on the cat (see page **151**)

Bandages

Bandages keep wounds clean and dry, reducing the chance of infection. They also protect against additional damage

Care of a Bandage

- Check for swelling and pus around the wound area. These are signs of infection
- Keep the cat indoors and quiet until healing is complete
- If it chews the bandage, put an Elizabethan collar on the cat (see page **151**)

Surgical Drains

Surgical drains are devices that allow pus and excess fluid to escape from a wound. This aids the healing process. They occasionally need to be cleaned in order to maintain efficiency. Do not be afraid to work with drains; they rarely hurt the cat when manipulated.

There are 2 common types of surgical drain. A loop drain is a loop of tape that goes through the skin and is closed with a knot.

A Penrose drain is a short piece of very soft plastic tube placed in the wound. One or both ends of the tube protrude from the skin. The fluid drains around the tube, not through it.

Care of a Surgical Drain

- Prepare the drain for cleaning
  - **Loop drains:** Pull the knot to the other end of the incision

  - **Penrose drains:** Wiggle the end of the drainage tube

- Remove excess pus and fluid from drainage holes
    - Soak some gauze with 3% hydrogen peroxide
    - Dab gauze over drainage holes to loosen dried pus and fluid
    - Remove pus and fluid

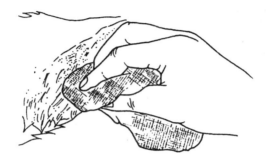

- Clean the drainage holes
    - Fill an eye dropper or syringe with 3% hydrogen peroxide
    - Squirt a small amount into the holes. (The peroxide will foam up)

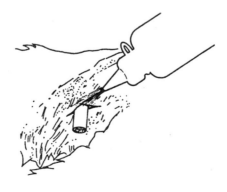

- Dab dry with gauze
- Repeat three times a day or as instructed by your veterinary surgeon
- If it chews the drain, put an Elizabethan collar on the cat

The Elizabethan Collar

An Elizabethan collar is a large plastic collar that fits around a cat's neck. It is named after a ruffle that people wore in the time of Queen Elizabeth I. It prevents the cat from pawing at its eyes and ears or from chewing at stitches, sores, splints, bandages and drains. Your veterinary surgeon will give you a collar if your cat needs to wear one.

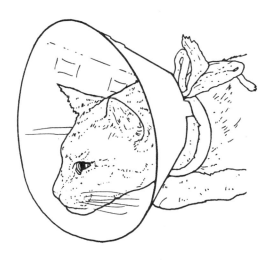

When placing a collar on your cat, fit it just tight enough so that it will not slip over the head. Use a strip of gauze to tie it on.

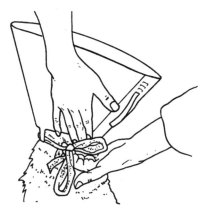

If your cat has had surgery around the face or ears, you may need to remove and clean the collar once a day.

26. Before and After Surgery

Overview

There may be times when it is in your cat's best interest to undergo surgery. There are steps you can take before and after the operation to help your cat. This chapter gives you some general guidelines. However, some operations require special preparation and care. Your veterinary surgeon will instruct you on the proper action.

Before Surgery

Preparing your Cat for Surgery

An operation may require that your cat be given an anaesthetic, which exposes it to a slight risk. When anaesthetised, a cat loses the protective reflex that closes the windpipe while swallowing. If it were to vomit, a portion may go down the windpipe and into the lungs. This could limit its capacity to breathe and may even result in death. You can help minimize this risk.

What to Do

• No food on the night before surgery.

What NOT to Do

- If you do feed your cat on the morning of the operation, do NOT hide this fact from your vet. It is better to delay surgery than to have a serious problem arise while under anaesthesia.

After Surgery

You will need to monitor your cat closely for a couple of weeks. Doing so will help ensure that proper healing occurs without complications.

The First 24 Hours

Most surgery takes place in the morning or early afternoon. The following steps assume that the operation took place then. Your veterinary surgeon will give you instructions on how to care for your cat during the first 24 hours.

- Do not give food until the morning after surgery. Until then, it will still be under some of the effects of the anaesthetic. Food may make it vomit. Access to water, however, is necessary
- Encourage rest. Keep the cat indoors in a dark, quiet area
- Do not touch wound unless instructed to do so
- Do not be alarmed if the wound bleeds a small amount. If there is profuse bleeding, call your veterinary surgeon immediately

Until the Stitches Come Out

Stitches normally come out 10 to 14 days after the surgery. The stitches that you can see are usually non-absorbable; your veterinary surgeon will remove them when appropriate. Stitches beneath the skin are usually absorbable. They will slowly disappear over the course of several weeks.

Until the stitches are taken out, you should watch your cat carefully. Its activities should be restricted; if not, the wound may open or tear. This could lead to another operation and a longer period of recovery.

- Keep the cat indoors
- Do not clean the wound unless instructed to do so
- Check the wound every day for swelling. It can be the result of several factors

  - **Reaction to Stitches:** this is the most common cause. The inflamed area does not diminish in size when pressed and it is usually not too painful or hot to the touch.

  - **Organs or Tissue Extending Through Incision:** abdominal surgery requires cutting through all of the muscle layers of the abdomen. Stitches that pull muscle layers together sometimes break down or pull apart, allowing abdominal organs and tissue to poke through and form a swelling under the skin. If you push this swelling, it will decrease in size. It usually does not feel hot. If a piece of white abdominal fat extends through the skin, do not pull it out; take your cat to your veterinary surgeon immediately.

- **Infection:** this is often hot to the touch with a thick creamy coloured discharge. The area usually cannot be reduced in size when pushed unless pus comes out between the stitches.

Contact Your Veterinary Surgeon if....

- There is any evidence of infection
- There is any swelling (unless it is obviously caused by the stitches alone)
- There is anything protruding from the wound
- There is a high body temperature (40°C [104°F] or above)
- The cat is not eating
- The cat is still very sleepy after 48 hours
- The cat is vomiting or has diarrhoea

References

AVMA Council on Biologic and Therapeutic Agents. "Canine and Feline Immunization Guidelines." *Journal of the American Veterinary Medical Association* (August 1,1989): 314-317.

Catcott, E.J., Ed., *Feline Medicine and Surgery, 2nd ed.* Santa Barbara, California: American Veterinary Publications, Inc., 1975.

Ettinger, Stephen J., *Textbook of Veterinary Internal Medicine: Disease of the Dog and Cat, 2nd ed.* Philadelphia: W.B. Saunders Company, 1983.

Holzworth, Jean, *Diseases of the Cat: Medicine and Surgery.* Philadelphia: W.B. Saunders Company, 1987.

Kirk, Robert W., *First Aid for Pets*. New York: E.P. Dutton, 1978.

Kirk, Robert W., Ed., *Current Veterinary Therapy VIII: Small Animal Practice*. Philadelphia: W. B. Saunders Company, 1983.

Kirk, Robert W., Ed., *Current Veterinary Therapy IX: Small Animal Practice*. Philadelphia: W. B. Saunders Company, 1986.

Kirk, Robert W., Ed., *Current Veterinary Therapy X: Small Animal Practice*. Philadelphia: W. B. Saunders Company, 1989.

Kirk, Robert W. and Stephen I. Bistner, *Handbook of Veterinary Procedures and Emergency Treatment, 4th ed.* Philadelphia: W. B. Saunders, 1985.

Pratt, Paul W., Ed., *Feline Medicine*. Santa Barbara, California: American Veterinary Publications, Inc., 1983.

Sherding, Robert G., Ed., *The Cat Diseases and Clinical Management*. New York: Churchill Livingstone Inc., 1989.

Siegmund, Otto H., et al., Eds., *The Merck Veterinary Manual, 5th ed.* Rahway, New Jersey: Merck & Co, Inc., 1979.

Urquhart, G.M., J. Armour, J.L. Duncan, A. M. Dunn and F.W. Jennings, *Veterinary Parasitology*. New York: Churchill Livingstone, Inc., 1987.

Index